Sitting Target

How and Why The Narcissist Chooses You

By

H G Tudor

All Rights Reserved

Copyright 2016

Sitting Target: How and Why the Narcissist Chooses You

By

HG Tudor

All rights reserved. No part of this book may be reproduced, stored in a retrieval system, or transmitted in any form or by any means, electronic, mechanical, photocopying, recording, or otherwise, without the express written permission of the publisher.

Published by Insight Books

1. Introduction

We never choose our victims at random. We engage in a careful and measured selection of those who we wish to draw into our world and serve our purposes. People put a lot of effort into choosing where they will live or the type of career that they will follow. We put plenty of effort, consideration and planning into choosing our victims. You may have performed the dance with the narcissist and now, having largely escaped, you may be wondering why you? Why were you chosen and treated like a queen and then thrown off the pedestal into the dirt below? Did the narcissist decide at the outset to subject you to this bewildering contrast in behaviours or were you just unlucky? You may still be in the grip of the narcissist and you are searching for answers as to what drew the narcissist to you in order to gain some understanding which will give you peace of mind and allow you to plot your escape. You may know someone you care about who has been targeted by our kind and you want to know why so you can reach out and help that friend or family member. Finally, you may belong to that rare group of people who knows about me and my kind and you want to ensure you see us coming. You want to know what it is that attracts our kind to your kind so that you can be vigilant and take steps to evade our clutches.

It may be the case you know other people who have fallen foul of our machinations. You may belong to a victim or survivor group where various war stories are swapped as horrific tales are exchanged about what has happened to each of you. Interestingly, many of these groups become little more than forums for two things; the detailing (sometimes on a day to day basis) of the abuse that is being doled out and a place to rail against the narcissist. Some clearly find it cathartic to explain in detail what the narcissist did to them today, or to ask others what their views are about the way the victim has been treated. Often these groups will go around in circles as the victim asks another, why is he doing this? What should I do? How do I make it stop? The bile and hatred for the narcissist is spewed forth and this entirely understandable. Pictures are created with the typically inspirational quote or message written underneath and posted in a valiant attempt to raise spirits and promote healing. Again this is all understandable and obviously has a value. However, I do not see these groups ever seeking to debate why each person was chosen. Many may think this to themselves but it does not tend to appear as something which is discussed. On the few occasions where it does, reference is made to the fact that the victims are empathic and are kind and decent people. Those are relevant and important traits but the simple fact is that these discussions do not get far because the victims do not really know why they have been selected. They do not understand the true nature as to why the narcissist picked them. Now you will be able to change that situation.

Did the narcissist choose you because you have green eyes or blue eyes or brown eyes? Did the narcissist choose you because of your job? The fact you have children or do not have children? Did he choose you because you have long hair or short cropped locks? Did he select you because of your choice of music, the nature of your favourite food or was it because you happened to be stuck in a lift together? Does the narcissist just choose anybody to be his victim and in reality has no discerning taste as to who he sinks his fangs into? Is it the case that anybody and everybody is a potential victim for the narcissist and everyone is at risk of becoming ensnared? I will be addressing considerations such as these.

I know from my vast experience that our victims, either when still in our clutches or surveying the aftermath of their tumultuous time with us will always wonder why me? I have written in other publications about how the need to know and understand is a central part of our victims' psyche. You need to understand why things happen so you can then choose the most appropriate step to take. You are also often burdened with guilt and in so many scenarios you will ask yourself whether you were to blame. You will analyse your behaviour and the dance you performed with us as you try and gain some kind of understanding as to what has happened. We know that you will obsess (because we make you do it) over every detail of what has happened. You will recall each day of your involvement with us and be able to recount the events, the things said and the action taken in considerable detail although you will not understand what has happened. You will consider whether you ought to have done something in a different fashion, if there was an alternative which may have brought about a change in the outcome. As you sit mulling these events over, debating them with your closest friends and family members, one question will keep manifesting in your mind; why me? Why did he or she choose me? What was it about me that meant he or she wanted me? Am I bad person? Did I deserve to be treated like this in some way? Did I bring it on myself? Was I naïve and missed certain clues as to this person's behaviour? Could I have done anything in a different way? Should I have listened more to what people were saying?

You may find yourself among a growing number of people who have been selected by our kind more than once. It is entirely common for this to happen. Some people do not realise that they have become enmeshed with one of our kind so that it happens a second and a third time. You may have been the victim of our kind through parental influence and then targeted by our kind in the context of a friendship or even more likely an intimate relationship. You ought to realise that being the victim of more than one narcissist is increasingly common. This is for reasons which I will expand on below.

Not only do you ponder why you were chosen but also you sit and look back and ask yourself, "How the hell did that happen?" How was it that one day you were making your way through life, attending to your home, carrying out your job and then some time later you were left devastated after being sucked into our false reality, spun around and around and then unceremoniously hurled to the wayside as we disappeared into the sunset arm in arm with our next victim? How did you get from confident and independent person to one who was truly suckered and mesmerised by our kind? How did we seek you out? How did we charm you in such a manner? How did we achieve all of this without you having any realisation as to what was actually going on? I won't be explaining how we charm and seduce – that is for elsewhere, but what I will be providing you with clarity, is how we went about selecting you and we went about getting into position to then advance our charm as we love bombed you into submission. Much of this will be complete news to you but by learning about it you will gain understanding which in turn will allow you to apply it for your own benefit and the benefit of others.

Whichever group you happen to belong to you are in the right place if you are looking for answers. You will not find lengthy scientific and psychological explanations here. There are plenty of texts accommodating those who wish to delve into the narcissist's world in that way, but they are often lengthy, rambling and fail to bridge the gap between the theory and the practical. This is not the case here. You have the distinct advantage of gaining this knowledge and information from a master practitioner of the dark art of narcissism. I am a narcissist. I have known this for some time as a consequence of my own intellect and also the repeated involvement of specialists who form part of my treatment, which is very much ongoing. As part of this treatment and also my desire to have an audience I have set down in writing many elements of the narcissistic lifestyle, worldview and behaviours in order to allow you to consider them and in turn gain a far better understanding of what we are and why we act as we do. Whilst victims and therapists provide a valuable role in aiding understanding and suggesting methods of recovery, they are not able to convey exactly what we think and why we act as we do, because they are not us. I am able to share with you my thoughts and actions, relay events which have happened in order to allow you to gain unrivalled access into the mind of the narcissist. This is not always comfortable reading but I am not going to pull any punches as to do so would insult you and we are not at that stage just yet! I will provide to you direct and uncompromising examples and explanations which will give you a level of understanding which you have not previously been able to access from other providers. I tell you exactly how it is, in terms which you can relate to and no doubt recognise but you never knew why the narcissist in your life behaved this way. That is all going to change as you delve into my world.

In this book I am going to explain to you why you were a sitting target, oblivious to what was coming your way. One of the key points which you will be able to take away from this book is the fact that you did nothing wrong. None of this was your fault. You were not "asking for it" when you were targeted by our kind and subsequently ensnared. You had no idea that you would be seduced and then devalued and there was no possible way you could escape it. You did not recognise what was pouring sugar into your ears and charming you so you had no hope for anticipating what was going to happen and even less of a hope of avoiding it. You should remind yourself that you are not at fault. You are blameless since, as you will read, the machinations of our kind mean you have no inkling of what we are doing. There was nothing you said or did which caused us to select you as our prey. It was not what you wore or what you drank which caused us to draw near to you. Conscious decisions you made had no impact on the fact that we wanted you.

By understanding how and why you were targeted you will be able to address the guilt that you feel. You will realise that you stood no chance because of the very fact you were not chosen at random. You were carefully chosen as a consequence of a considered campaign to identify you as best serving our needs. Once selected we were then able to apply our charm and seduction, our manipulation to you in order to bring about the result we required. In essence, your fate was sealed the moment that we saw you and decided that we would ascertain whether you would give us what we want. Someone like you, for reasons which will become apparent, will always attract our kind. You are the single light in the darkness which, like moths, we will flock to. You are the sole source of water in a vast desert and your spring is where we parched individuals must drink deep from. You stand out to people like us. You are highlighted and exposed. There is now way, when you are unaware of just how attractive you are to us, for you to escape out attentions. It is only when you realise and moreover understand how and why we chose you that you can look for our advances. You may not be able to stop our approach from happening, as we tend to exhibit considerable enthusiasm for ensnaring you, but you will know what is happening and then be in a far better position to make the correct decisions which allow you to escape our snaking tendrils before they have begun to take a hold on you.

I will explain to you the types of target that we concern ourselves with, why those targets are so attractive to us and then the hunting grounds which we stalk in order to find your kind. Once you have been located I will detail the preparatory work which we engage in, in order to bring about your seduction, the green lights that tell us our targeting is correct and how you will eventually succumb to our onerous overtures. I will explain to you what it is that we want from you and why you, above anyone else is in the best possible position to provide those things for you. I will allow you to understand how we approach our victims and how our tendrils wrap around you so you have no chance to escape us. Most of all I will allow you to understand, finally, how you are a sitting target and how and why I chose you as my victim.

You are most likely reading this because you have suffered since you have been in a relationship, of an intimate nature, with a narcissist. That is where the most damage is done. This is because those who are enmeshed with us in the intimate sense are those who are at greatest risk of being abused since intimate partners are usually (although not exclusively) those who are subjected to our cycle of seduction, devaluation, discard and then Hoover. There are other categories of what I refer to as Proximity of Supply (the closeness and nature of the victim's relationship with the narcissist) who may be subjected to this cycle but often many categories, outside of the intimate relationship, are only subjected to seduction. This is because those other people, friends, family members, colleagues, minions, acquaintances and so on have a role to play in believing our façade, that we are a kind, decent, interesting and honest person. We do not ever want this façade to be destroyed for two main reasons. One the maintenance of the façade enables us to continue to draw positive fuel from those who believe in it. Thus, the people who think we are wonderful will continue to provide positive fuel by admiring us, loving us, telling us how special we are, how good we are at our jobs and so forth. We want that to continue. The second reason is to have ranks of people who will all testify to our good nature, so that should you try and smear our good name when we are devaluing you and especially once we have discarded you, you will not be believed. You will be regarded as jealous, spiteful and hateful. All of which will provide us with more fuel as you rant and rave about how awful we are and how blinded those who look upon the façade are. It also allows us to maintain a grip on you, in readiness for our Hoover, by keeping you bewildered and disorientated. Thus, those who look on the façade are not often subjected to devaluation. This can happen where, say a friend, fails to keep up the supply of fuel, or they listen to your overtures and start to become disloyal or they criticise us (which as you know we hate) but in the main those who are needed to look on the façade will only ever find themselves in the seduction stage. It is of course entirely different for you by virtue of the fact that you were chosen as our intimate partner and you are on the receiving end of astonishing love bombing, horrendous devaluation, callous discard and then ferocious Hoover. Your susceptibility to the manipulative techniques which we deploy during these stages is also a factor in why you have been selected by us and I detail more of that in later chapters.

Central, as it always is, to our behaviours is our need for fuel. If you have not already done so I recommend you read my book **Fuel** as this will set out for you in detail why fuel is so important to us, how we get it and your role in all of this amongst many other enlightening topics. I will frequently explain below how fuel affects why and how you have been targeted by the narcissist but you will see that whilst it is the main consideration it is not the sole consideration as there are other important factors which come into play as well when we are considering whether to target you or not.

I have little doubt that as you read on your will experience that shudder of familiarity and many of the instances that I shall describe. I also know that you will be alarmed and horrified at the manner in which you have been targeted and how ruthlessly clinical our behaviour is. You should always keep in mind that whilst we chose you because of the way you are, it is not personal, since there are many people who could be chosen and they would fulfil the same role as you did. You happened to come within our sights at a particular time and because of what you are, you attracted our attention immediately. Whilst it is the case that many of your traits and attributes drew us to you, the reality is that you were selected because of what we are and our thirst. The cold manner in which we selected you should not be regarded as any reflection on you but is entirely indicative of the manner in which we approach this task. It is a process for us. It is mechanical and devoid of emotion on our part. Of course, much of the reason why you were chosen concerns emotion, but that is on your side and not ours. Read on and finally gain understanding as to why and how you were chosen by your narcissist.

2. The Type of Target

The methodology of our selection of our target is governed, initially, by two considerations.

1. What we are; and
2. The role we wish to fill.

These two considerations will then cause us to target certain people on the basis that they will be the optimum person for our needs. In terms of what we are, of course we are a narcissist and you will be familiar with the various traits by which we are defined as being that personality type. Not all of those traits are present with every narcissist and whilst it is worthwhile you being aware of those traits it is far more important for you to recognise the type of narcissist that you may have been involved with and perhaps even more importantly the type or possibly types that may target you in the future. Some of our victims satisfy us whatever type of narcissist we are whereas others are more suited to a particular type thus certain of our kind will not bother targeting that victim. I have explained elsewhere the types of narcissist which exist but it will do you no harm to familiarise yourself again with these types in order to ensure you fully understand how our targeting works.

Narcissists are drawn from two schools and what I refer to as four cadres. The schools are those of being of a Lesser variety, Mid-Range Variety or a Greater variety. The cadres are the Victim, the Somatic, the Cerebral and the Elite Narcissist. Narcissists belong to both a school and a cadre although there is not a category of narcissist for every combination of school and cadre as some are mutually exclusive. It is necessary for you to understand not only the schools and cadres but also the relevant combinations. This is for the following reasons: -

1. You will understand what to expect from the behaviour of the relevant class of narcissist;

2. This will shape the way he or she targets their victims, since different classes look for different traits in their victims;
3. The further content of this book will make much greater sense (and thus in turn assist you) since you understand the classes of narcissist that exist; and
4. You will have a greater understanding of why the narcissist is drawn to you so you can take the appropriate action.

Ascertain the type of narcissist you have been involved in from the detail provided below, but also keep in mind the other types that exist because we will also be examining what each type looks for dependent on the particular class of narcissist.

The Schools

The Lesser Narcissist

The Lesser Narcissist is typically low functioning. He is unlikely to know what he is and will reject any suggestion that he is a narcissist, instead retreating into blame shifting and projection. The Lesser Narcissist has just as great a need for fuel as any other narcissist but will always take the path of least resistance to obtain this fuel. The Hoover from a Lesser Narcissist will neither be intense nor will it be sustained once he recognises that he is facing considerable resistance. He will instead seek out a new primary source of fuel instead as this will be easier. He has no desire to seek near annihilation of his victims and instead once discarded only Hoover should they present the opportunity on a plate for him to do so. The Lesser Narcissist has lower energy levels and is very much a creature of economy. He sees little to be gained in higher stake approaches even if the promise of the fuel should such an approach succeed be fantastic. He would rather find an easier route. It is not the case that he or she is not a risk-taker but it turns on the fact that they cannot in fact be bothered to chase difficult (albeit more rewarding fuel) and will instead take it from easy sources. They classically always look for the low hanging fruit.

The Mid-Range Narcissist

The Mid-Range Narcissist possesses a reasonable level of functioning. He will work harder than a Lesser Narcissist to achieve his aims and will push harder when Hoovering but he lacks the superior attributes of the Greater Narcissist and does not share the malign intent that the Greater Narcissist is known for. The Mid-Range Narcissist will engage in sustained Hoovers and will look further afield than a Lesser Narcissist to do so. The Mid-Range Narcissist is usually identified by reason of omission. They do not exhibit the incandescent fury, malign intent and utter driven nature of the Greater Narcissist. By contrast they do not either show the economy of approach nor the lesser functioning ability of the Lesser Narcissist. Accordingly, if the narcissist that you have entangled with does not show any Lesser or Greater traits then you can safely place him or her as a Mid-Range Narcissist.

The Greater Narcissist

The Greater Narcissist (sometimes known as the malign narcissist) is a high functioning individual. This narcissist will be well aware of what he or she does and the nature of its impact yet has no regard for the chaos caused or the collateral damage generated. The Greater Narcissist can be identified by virtue of increased energy levels, the greater intensity of the Hoover, the sustaining of a longer period of Hoover and an all-pervading malevolence. The Greater Narcissist will look to crush his or her victim to near obliteration in the ruthless pursuit of punishment. The Lesser Narcissist has no interest in punishment. The Mid-Range will achieve punishment if little effort is required. The Greater Narcissist has punishment very much on his or her agenda and will readily expend considerable energies in achieving this so long as sufficient fuel exists to support such a campaign. The Greater Narcissist has a more expansive manipulative toolkit and is capable of wreaking extensive harm to those who cross his or her path. A Greater Narcissist, if he so chooses, could readily seduce a Lesser Narcissist although naturally such a step would be fuel-limited and the categories of empathic individual, super empathic individual and co-dependent are vastly preferred.

Accordingly, these different schools of narcissist will have different considerations when targeting their victims. Certain traits in those victims will prove more appealing to particular narcissists and we will address this in more detail below. By way of an early example however, a narcissist from the Lesser School will look for somebody who has an accommodating and compliant personality so he or she does not have to expend much energy is both seducing this victim and thereafter extracting fuel by way of devaluation. As a contrast, the Greater Narcissist will readily want a strong and independent individual who will provide him with a challenge. The Greater Narcissist will welcome this opportunity to demonstrate to the victim that he or she is truly superior by bringing someone who exhibits a feistiness and an independent will, to heel. The Greater Narcissist has more energy available to him or her to achieve this and the pay-off is the increased quality of fuel which is provided by someone with traits such as independence and significant will power. We will delve into this in more detail presently. This does however allow you to begin to understand why your particular narcissist chose you.

Turning now to the cadres. By way of reminder there are four. Victim, Cerebral, Somatic and Elite. We address the Victim Narcissist first.

Victim Narcissist

All narcissists play at being the victim at some point but not all narcissists are of the victim variety. Non-victim narcissists are content to use their perception of victim hood by virtue of manipulating their targets and victims. Furthermore, they will use their perception as being a victim for the purposes of driving their desire to act against people. Non-victim narcissists use the concept of being a victim as device and place it on themselves and remove it at will like a mask. True Victim Narcissists adopt a permanent state of being a victim both in outlook and behaviour. They regard the world as a place whereby they have been denied their rightful inheritance of looks, intellect, wealth and power and instead they rely on others to provide it to them instead. The Victim Narcissist will look to others to repair his failings such as lack of money, lack of home, lack of job and overall lack of competence. Here are some earlier indicators of the characteristics that the Victim Narcissist will be looking for in those that he or she targets. He will not look for his narcissism to be fixed because he is unaware of what he is since the Victim Narcissist is low functioning and can only be from the school of lesser narcissism.

Should you become entangled with a Victim Narcissist he or she may lash out at you. Indeed, owing to their low functioning, physical abuse ranks higher as a manipulative tool with these individuals. The need to bully through physical violence means that a Victim Narcissist will be looking for a physically inferior target, one who cannot fight back or if he or she does, they can easily be bested. This lashing out however is not borne of a malign nature because the Victim Narcissist lacks both the capability and desire to behave in a malign way. You will not find a Victim Narcissist who is malign.

The Victim Variety of narcissist is somebody who lacks the body and looks obsession of the somatic narcissist and also lacks the intellect of the cerebral narcissist. He is typically a low-functioning narcissist since he does not inherently have the wit or intelligence to seduce his victims through words and demonstrations of intellectual brilliance. Neither does he have the drive or discipline to take care of himself physically, dress well, and have a rigorous hygiene and looks maintenance ritual. He is however a narcissist and needs to seduce his victims all the same and he does so by presenting as a victim who needs looking after.

They also do not tend to love-bomb hugely effectively but instead they merely hide their savage side in the initial stages so they are at least not off-putting. I also tend to think that they draw their victims in not by a show of supremacy and strength but rather by eliciting sympathy. They play on the empath's sense of caring and nurturing and present as a victim in order to be mothered by the empath. Accordingly, they do not exhibit the same degree of allure, charisma and all around sparkling brilliance as we do. They are still able to draw people in because there are caregivers who do not care so much about how someone looks and so on, but feel sorry for them and want to care for them and make them better. Similarly, in sexual matters they exhibit no brilliance between the sheets and may even demonstrate incompetence in order to draw further sympathy and invite the caring empath to teach them to be better. These narcissists are entirely self-centred and lack the charm and tools to draw their victims in with brilliance and magnificence. These narcissists do tend to be from the lower functioning variety that is not especially good at anything. They will provide some embellishment but again because they are low- functioning they will lack the intelligence, guile and wit to conjure up fantastic tales of achievement and accomplishment. Instead, they need to keep their abusive streak in check, something they are able to do but they need to find some other way of drawing in their victims. They cannot hold up anything shiny or sparkling in the way that most of our kind does. Instead, they do the reverse. What they exhibit is rusting, battered and dented but they do it in a "Shucks look at me, I am in a bit of a mess, and I need someone to help me out, would that kind person be you?" They present their victim status very early on and this will not be attractive to many people but it will draw certain people to them, those who want to care for them, mother them and make them become better. The Victim Narcissist often lacks any financial resources, may not be employed (and if he or she is they will be in a low-skilled occupation) and will relish the opportunity to forgo working so that the victim can support them. This type of narcissist has no interest in status unlike say an Elite Narcissist, but instead their sense of entitlement will outweigh any concerns about status. You should look after them if you say you love them. They are entitled to be cared for by reason of the fact that they are victims. They will regard themselves as a bit of a rough diamond, which needs polishing up and the empathic victim they have selected is just the person to do this.

Since this type of narcissist does not rely on being a shining beacon of attraction to people but rather a battered old vehicle which needs some tender loving care he sees no reason to let the flattery flow. There is little in the way of grandiose gestures or extravagance. Instead he will just play the victim card repeatedly in order to keep that empath looking after him and drawn to him. He is appreciative of the attention and caring and why not? He is gaining fuel but is also being looked after. He will probably not work and rely on the financial ability of the victim in that respect. He will help a little, just enough to avoid reprimand and enough to draw thanks from the empath. He keeps the abuse in check and therefore whilst never over the top in word or gesture he is pleasant enough. He certainly is not horrible His gratitude at being looked after and given attention by the empath satisfies the empath and they are willing to overlook the deficiencies because they feel good about taking care of this person. Since this type of narcissist has no need to look good, sound great and shine this attitude pervades into the sexual arena. He need not make his partner feel orgasmic and on a higher place. She will just be grateful he made the effort. In that way that all empaths make excuses she will regard his ineptitude between the sheets as just another item that makes him seem lovable and charming. Okay, he is not the world's best lover, he is not even in the top thousand but he tries and that is all the empath in such a relationship, as this, will want. The empath may just be happy to have someone to share his or her life with and care for. They are not scintillating like me and others that are like me. Accordingly, therefore being a sexual superstar is unnecessary. As I have mentioned in other writings, we are not only creatures of economy but we have been created economically. We do not like to expend energy unnecessarily. It is also the case that if it is not going to gather us fuel we do not need it. In the way that we are not furnished with empathy or the capacity for the remorse, because they do not gather any fuel for us, the low functioning Victim Narcissist is not blessed with sexual prowess, as it serves no purpose for him. He will only seek out those that want to mother him. He will not seek out those who want to be taken to sexual nirvana repeatedly. He will not need to use this sexual weapon to charm his victim because his helplessness and victim status does that for him instead. Accordingly, many of these low functioning narcissists either have little interest in sex or are useless at it.

Sex is still a material factor in the relationship with the Victim Variety because he will exhibit incompetence in this arena so that the caring empath feels sorry for him and will even feel a need to try and teach him. Some narcissists who are of the Victim Variety will go even further and demonstrate varying degrees of frigidity. Once again, this is designed to draw out sympathy from the empath. It is also done to garner sexual attention as well. By exhibiting no interest or little interest in sex or even appearing impotent, the desire to fix will be overwhelming for the empath who will do her best to try to light the fire of desire in this low-functioning narcissist.

The Victim Narcissist will often present with illnesses and ailments. He does not enjoy good health, which is a consequence of him rarely partaking in exercise and his inability to look after himself properly in terms of nutrition and/or hygiene. Not only will he appear with numerous ongoing physical health complaints he will typically invent additional ones in order to draw sympathy and evade having to do things. He has repeated bad backs, injured knees, depression, headache and the like. He is a malingerer and if he cannot point to one of his many ongoing complaints he will readily invent one in order to ensure that the empathic individual that he has ensnared will continue to care for him. You can guarantee that the Victim Narcissist when performing a Hoover (albeit of low intensity and not for a sustained period) will always use the Emergency Power Play and/or the Victim Power Play as part of his portfolio.

You will always find Lesser Victim Narcissists but never any Greater Victim Narcissists. There are occasional Mid-Range Victim Narcissists but the vast majority hail from the lesser school.

The Cerebral Narcissist

The Cerebral Narcissist has a limited interest in sex, certainly of the physical variety. This type of narcissist prefers to flaunt his brilliant intellect as the method by which he seduces his victims. He has little interest in engaging in actual sexual relations because that is not his forte. He has no interest in a remarkable physical appearance because he has no need of it. He need not be toned or slim although it does not always follow that the cerebral narcissist neglects his body to the extent that he becomes some kind of slob. After all, he has suitable awareness and intellect to understand the problems arising from the neglect of his health. He will not be an Adonis but it does not follow that he will be morbidly obese and of questionable hygiene habits. His magnificence stems from his high intellect, his amazing memory and his capacity for complexity. It is the repeated tales of academic achievement, cerebral power and scintillating intellect, which are used to wow and overpower the resistance of his victims. The cerebral narcissist is well read, extensively schooled and excels in showering all who will listen with evidence of his intellectual superiority. Such brilliance proves highly attractive to a certain section of empathic individuals who wish to engage a brain that is the size of a planet. The conversations, albeit one-sided, are nevertheless stimulating and engrossing. There is never a silence for the cerebral narcissist is always primed to provide you with an interesting fact about the champagne that you are both drinking and a historical anecdote concerning the Ponte Vecchio that you are walking over. This walking almanac of facts and opinions is quite dazzling and vastly appealing to some.

The cerebral narcissist will engage in sex periodically if the intellectual avenue becomes exhausted. The sex will not be fulfilling for either party owing to the fact that the cerebral narcissist is neither interested in this nor particularly proficient. It will be done when the intellectual charm is not working as well as it once did and is often done out of a sense of obligation. The cerebral narcissist will feel that every so often he is obligated to discharge his marital responsibilities by engaging in sex with his partner. This is purely done in order to maintain the happiness of the other individual during the golden period and during devaluation, the cerebral narcissist will effectively become frigid, as he will have no interest or sense of obligation to engage in sexual relations with his victim.

The cerebral narcissist however will often talk about sex during the seduction stage. Words are very much the weapons of the narcissist and especially so with the higher functioning of our kin. The cerebral narcissist although uninterested in the physical side of sex, will still wish to show off his vast knowledge of the subject. He will want to regale you with his knowledge of sexual literature, sexual analysis and sexual awareness. He will have read many books about the subject. That is not to enable him to be a better lover but to allow him to be a better speaker about being a lover. The cerebral narcissist will engage in seductive letter writing, often of the old school romantic variety. He will tease and titillate using text messages and telephone messages. He will quite readily, purely for the purpose of seduction, talk dirty down the telephone to you whilst you masturbate. He may tell you he is doing the same but he will not as the physical sensation is of no interest to him. What arouses him is the intellectual power he has in being able to use his lexicon of love to arouse you down the telephone line. Your noises of appreciation and compliments provide him with the fuel he requires, he demonstrates how knowledgeable he is about sex by talking in this manner and he has the added bonus of not having to engage in the actual act. This suits the cerebral narcissist most well. There will be plenty of opportunities for him to exhibit his wide knowledge of sexual practices in order to heighten your anticipation and to wow you as you listen wide-eyed to his explanations of certain techniques and behaviours and what they achieve. He knows all about sex but he certainly does not put it into practice. That is beneath him. In the way that those with a suntan were once looked down upon because this denoted being a manual labourer, the cerebral narcissist looks down on the actual sexual act as beneath him. Why engage in something so crass, something so animalistic and frankly barbaric (other than out of a sense of occasional duty to maintain the façade of the golden period) when one can use the pristine cleanliness of a beautiful mind to gain that all-important fuel? I have a cousin who is a little younger than I am. He is the offspring of my Uncle Peter (who you can read all about in **Fury**) and has been created in the same way as Uncle Peter but he does not have the interest in sex preferring to use his excellent academic credentials and brilliant mind to effect his acquisition of fuel. My cousin finds the act of sexual intercourse so abhorrent because he sees it as beneath someone with such a fine mind as him that on the few occasions he has been compelled to do it, he runs off to the bathroom afterwards and vomits. Not only does he not like the intimacy that comes with the act of coitus but the noise, the fluids, the interaction of parts from which one urinates all disgusts him as he has told me, to my amusement, on many occasions.

The Cerebral Narcissist places significant weight on his intellect being lauded and recognised. He excels in sitting and passing exams and will have a string of qualifications in order to brow beat any opponent before the debate has begun. He is more qualified ergo he is superior. The Cerebral Narcissist places considerable value on his intellectual achievements being recognised and any failure to do so will ignite his fury. He cannot stand ignorance. He will correct people when they speak, revel in revealing they are incorrect about a fact and love nothing more than to hold forth and argue with people. For him more than any other cadre narcissist words are the essence of his being. He loves the economy that accompanies their use, he delights in the effect they have both in seduction and devaluation and his superiority must always be recognised.

The Cerebral Narcissist, in the same way that he is disinterested in his body and the sexual arena, has no interest in physical abuse. It will take a severe loss of control, possibly on entering the Chaos Mode or alternatively following sustained criticisms whereby the fury is ignited, for a Cerebral Narcissist to use physical abuse against his or her victim. It will tend to be grabbing, pushing and holding down as opposed to punching and kicking. The Cerebral Narcissist is also aware of the evidential ramifications arising from physical abuse and is too clever (unless control has been lost) to engage in such behaviours. He regards physical abuse as beneath him, preferring to engage in the fine art of emotional and psychological abuse.

The Cerebral Narcissist is an extensive user of Lieutenants. His innate charisma combined with his intellect enables him to recruit and manipulate others. Since he shuns the body, he prefers others to do the donkeywork and is entirely content to recruit them to do this on his behalf. He will carry out much of his work by proxy, seeing it as beneath him to become involved in the minutiae of the abuse but rather he is there to plan it, orchestrate it and command it.

Naturally you will not find any Lesser Cerebral Narcissists. They are drawn both from the ranks of the Mid-Range school whereby the Cerebral Narcissist will exhibit all the traits explained above but will lack any malign intent. Those Greater Cerebral Narcissists are dangerous individuals. Their higher function combined with their emphasis on the mind mean that all manner of manipulative tools will be used against you during seduction and devaluation. The Greater Cerebral Narcissist is Machiavellian in approach, covert and extremely manipulative. All narcissists lie but he is the Chief of Lies. Words are his speciality and it follows that in unleashing his malevolent campaign against you lies will be used extensively. In fact, it is fair to say that he will issue more untruths than truth and thus makes for a most dangerous opponent.

The Somatic Narcissist

Here comes the gym bunny that has a bottom so tight it will bounce off the walls before he bounces you all around the bedroom. The Somatic Narcissist is obsessed with his or her physical appearance. They diet fastidiously, put the hours in at the gym, select the clothing which allows them to flaunt their bodies and spend a lot of time with their favourite person; their reflection in the mirror. They look for reactions of admiration to their beauty, their physical perfection, their muscular appearance and smart and attractive appearances. The Somatic Narcissist likes to demonstrate athletic ability by showing his body can throw the furthest, run the fastest or dive the deepest. The appearance of his or her body and what can be achieved through it (strength, flexibility, and endurance) are what matter in order to draw fuel from their victims.

This fixation with the body means that the arena of sex is hugely important to the Somatic Narcissist. He wants to look terrific whilst having sex so you coo and purr over that finely honed body, the impressive biceps and rigid six-pack. Not only that but look at how he can have sex for a long time as he flips you from this position to the next like a piece of meat. His stamina is legendary, his ability to get you and him into all manner of positions should be respected and admired and all of this is achieved whilst looking like a Greek god. Whereas the cerebral narcissist uses his intellect to conquer, the somatic narcissist uses his or her body to achieve the same outcome. His body is designed for admiration and where better to achieve that than in the bedroom.

The Somatic Narcissist will also demonstrate the legendary hypocrisy for which we are known. You must not compete with him in any way in the looks department but you are expected to look your best because you are an extension of him. You must not gain weight, have bad skin, wear ill-fitting clothes or forget to shave your legs. You must walk the tightrope of ensuring that you fit in with his image of bodily perfection whilst at the same time not pulling the spotlight away from him. The Somatic Narcissist will excel during the seductive stage because the twin allure of somebody looking so good and performing so brilliantly between the sheets will blow you away. You will receive premium quality sex, amazing orgasms and a grade A sexual encounter. His stamina is vast, his eagerness and readiness to copulate is staggering and you will be the beneficiary in all of this. This is just a fortunate coincidence for you because as with all types of our kind, the Somatic Narcissist is just after your fuel. You may not regard this as such a problem during the seduction phase. So what if he gets off on your screams of pleasure and your repeated appreciation of those defined forearms and pectoral muscles, you are being given the sexual time of your life, he deserves the praise doesn't he? Naturally, this is how we want it to work. You give us the fuel, have no realisation what you are doing, and therefore have no concern, so consequently you embrace it wholeheartedly. When the devaluation occurs, you can expect the somatic narcissist to maintain still a rampant sexual appetite but the last thing on his mind will be making you purr with pleasure. You will be taken against your will, subjected to lengthy sexual hammerings as he focuses on how brilliant he is at lasting so long, how glorious his taut muscles look as he ploughs away at you. There is no consideration for whether you are enjoying yourself or even if you are being physically hurt because all that matters to him is how good he looks and how masterful he is in the sack. If you were to vanish from beneath him, he would barely notice. The somatic narcissist is in effect having sex with himself. He is so fine to look at that he would eat himself if he could and similarly he would engage in sexual intercourse with himself if that were a possibility. Masturbation ranks high with narcissists anyway but this action is even more prevalent with the somatic narcissist. He will position himself in front a mirror and as he plays with himself, he will admire how he looks and this reinforces his need for you to admire him also. The somatic narcissist will bombard you with pictures of his buff body and his penis during the seduction stage. He will also do this with online strangers in order to gain their admiration also.

Exhibiting their physicality is necessary for the somatic variety of our kind. Accordingly, you can expect sexual gymnastics during the seduction phase and then to be slapped, smacked, bent over, throttled, pinned down and all other manifestations of physical dominance. The fear in your eyes as he pins you to the bed and takes what he regards as his only goes to fuel him further. Any kind of treatment, which emphasises his physical prowess and superiority, will be meted out in the sexual arena and invariably you will suffer consequently. You can expect to be humiliated, dominated and shoved around by the somatic narcissist during devaluation. You are little more than a blow-up doll to him, which is to be manipulated into all manner of positions all in order to make him look magnificent. You are expected to be grateful for the sexual pounding you have received and if your praise is not forthcoming then expect the consequences, as this inherent criticism will ignite his rage. Rather than rely on withering put downs and caustic comments, the somatic narcissist will lash out physically, again underpinning his physical superiority whilst storing away your transgression for use in the sexual arena at a later date. The somatic narcissist will insist on bondage, your subjugation being a natural consequence of his superiority. You will be bent over his knee and smacked with his hand or a cane. I know of one narcissist who would apply nettles to his scrotum because he explained it gave him a massive and sustained erection, notwithstanding the pain and he expected his victim to endure the application of those nettles to her nipples, bottom and thighs in order to heighten her sexual experience also. In the hands of the somatic narcissist, sex is a highly charged weapon. It is with the somatic narcissist that you will experience the greatest highs during the sexual seduction and the humiliating and hurtful lows when the devaluation occurs.

The Somatic Narcissist lets his or body do the talking and therefore words whilst used by the Somatic Narcissist are used less extensively and with less impact than if they were being wielded by the Cerebral Narcissist. You will find that much of what the Somatic Narcissist will say will revolve around how magnificent he or she looks, material items, his or new car, the new house they have bought or the new extension to a house. The material and the tangible are what matter to the Somatic Narcissist and accordingly money, expensive items and events are high on their list of priorities. It is all about how it looks. They like to appear magnificent both in their appearance and the environment in which they operate. They are the epitome of showing off the shiny and the sparkling as part of their approach to seduce and beguile you. During devaluation you can expect all of the beautiful things to be withdrawn and for their words to focus on how you have lost your looks, gained weight, how you are not caring about your appearance anymore, that you are failing to keep the house tidy and such like. Much of what the Somatic Narcissist will say will revolve around appearance and presentation.

There are no Lesser Somatic Narcissists. Their lack of interest in their environment, lower functioning and general poor physical appearance and health do not equate to the Somatic Narcissist. The Mid-Range Somatic Narcissist is still rampant in their sexual appetite, their desire for all to look beautiful and their obsession with looks. They will however lack the drive and malignant nature of the Greater Somatic Narcissist. This creature is a lady-killer or a seductive siren. Utterly vain, compellingly beautiful or handsome he or she knows that to look upon them is to look upon the beauty of heaven. They regard their beauty as captivating. They turn heads, stop traffic and have people fall in love with them from the moment they set eyes on him or her. The Greater Somatic Narcissist has an incredible sexual appetite from the get go and uses this to stun their victim into submission. By equal turns they will wrench it away from their victim once the malign nature is unleashed. The Greater Somatic Narcissist is a cruel creature, entranced by their own image and someone who is all too ready to lambaste others who fall beneath their ridiculously high standards. The Greater Somatic Narcissist is an occasion when beauty has never been so ugly.

The Elite Narcissist

The final category of narcissist is the Elite Narcissist. He combines both the looks and physical supremacy of the Somatic Narcissist with the intellect and spoken charm of the Cerebral Narcissist. The Elite Narcissist will talk you into bed and deliver as well. He will have your mind aroused and then your body. He may not be quite the sexual champion that the Somatic Narcissist is but he is no slouch. He will look after himself and be trim and athletic if not ripped and buff, but such a look is not beyond him. He may not have the total cranial magnificence of the Cerebral Narcissist but again he is no dribbling idiot. He has plenty of intelligence and wit, which he puts to good use. This combination of intelligence and looks creates the deadliest narcissist because he can use to both charm and seduce you and then use both to devalue you. Hence, he is categorised as an elite member of our club.

The Elite Narcissist is interested in sex because he recognises that sex comes in many forms. He knows that is can be the sensual whisper in your ear or the raunchy text messaging he sends you. He knows it is the athletic and sudden performance in a penthouse suit and the gentle, tender lovemaking that you crave. He has none of the disgust for the sexual act like the Cerebral Narcissist and does not rely solely on physical domination like the Somatic Narcissist. He is able to combine both worlds and straddle the same in order to exact his manipulations. Where the mouth leads, his body will follow and you are subjected to the one-two combination. Whilst the Victim Narcissist needs the mothering empath, the Cerebral Narcissist needs the disciple empath who worships at this temple of knowledge, the Somatic Narcissist needs the empath who is swayed by looks, and the Elite Narcissist just needs somebody with empathic qualities. They may not be a complete empath but the everyday charm and attractiveness of the Elite Narcissist will seduce someone who may have lower empathic qualities than normal and this in turn provides the Elite Narcissist with access to a larger pool of potential victims. Naturally, the Elite Narcissist will be using sex (in word and deed) to ensnare an empath, a super-empath or a co-dependent but he is able to mine fuel from some of the lesser prospects. The Elite Narcissist will use the spoken charm and knowledge of the Cerebral Narcissist and meld it with the sexual physical allure of the Somatic Narcissist to create a very potent sexual magnet indeed. Few can resist him and the sex he grants is gratifying on many levels. For the same reason, when the Elite Narcissist commences the devaluation, his victim his subjected to a further double whammy as spoken word and physical act are used against her. The effect is devastating.

The Elite Narcissist stalks the world with his double-barrel of capabilities to charm and ensnare and when the time is right he can turn that double-barrel on his victim and unleash not one but two forms of devastating devaluation. This cadre of narcissist is very difficult to resist. Although it may look like an oxymoron there are Mid-Range Elite Narcissists. This means that those who combine looks and intellect do so with particular effect but they do so without the drive and malign intent of those from the Greater school. They perform effective Hoovers, which are sustained and intense because the Elite Narcissist has combined two cadres of narcissist, which gives him or her more tools to apply, more manipulations to administer and a greater prospect of ensnaring their victim once again. Those that are without the malign influence will move on to a different victim should the current target exhibit a slavish devotion to No Contact.

Ultimately there is the Greater Elite Narcissist. This malevolent and malign creature will seduce you with a double whammy of looks and intellect, whisk you off your feet in seconds and be the toast of everyone you know. You will be regarded as having secured the golden ticket to the golden period and in utter nirvana. As ever the higher you climb the greater your fall and when the Greater Elite Narcissist unleashes his or campaign of vitriolic devaluation against you, you will need to get far away if you are ever to escape him or her. The Grand Hoover deployed by the Greater Elite Narcissist is of hurricane force as every conceivable method of manipulation is hurled at you in a fearsome bid to cause you to capitulate. Even if, somehow, you manage to survive the Grand Hoover you will be subjected to repeated attempts to draw you back in. No matter what other fuel the Greater Elite Narcissist has acquired he or she will still dedicate time and energy to your downfall. They will not rest until one day they have secured that potent Hoover fuel from you. It may be tomorrow of in fifteen years but they will always come after you.

Accordingly, these are the classes of narcissist which you need to be aware of and below I will detail what it is that each class looks for in their target so you are aware as to why you are the target of this particular narcissist. At the outset of this chapter I explained that our methodology is governed by what we are, namely the class of narcissist but also the role that we must have fulfilled. This is where you become relevant. In terms of the role, the overriding objective of course is the provision of fuel and this means that the role is divide into two distinct categories:
-

1. The Primary Source of Fuel; and
2. Supplementary Sources

The Primary Source of Fuel

This is the category that you are most likely to belong to if you are reading this book. Those who are in this category have the greatest exposure to us, experience the elation of the sustained seduction which goes beyond anything anyone in the supplementary source category would ever experience and you also then face the horror of the devaluation, the bewilderment of discard and the lure of the Hoover. You were chosen because we determined that you would fulfil the role of the primary source especially well because we ascertained when we targeted you that you would provide fuel on a frequent basis, of a high-grade and in copious amounts. This determination is linked to what type of narcissist we are and I will explain which of your traits most you most suitable for the position of primary source with your particular narcissist. The fundamental point to understand is that those chosen for this role must always be an intimate partner. There may be occasions when, owing to urgency and a lack of available options, this role might be filled with a family member or a friend but that is rare. The intimate partner is always preferred in the role of primary source. There are several reasons for this: -

1. You spend the most time with us out of all the people we interact with and therefore you are best placed to provide us with fuel more frequently than anyone else;
2. You have been chosen because you believe in love and the attraction of being in a relationship. You place great value in these things and therefore you will give a heightened emotional response. You want to be in a relationship so you will give more to it, you will work harder to make it work and preserve it. You will be more loving, more appreciative and more admiring. Similarly, when devaluation occurs you will experience hurt on a greater level, frustration, upset and anger and accordingly your emotional response and thus fuel will be far greater;
3. We will invariably reside with you, either by spending time at your house or my house together a lot of the time or by moving in together. This will enable us to maintain the façade whilst mete out our less desirable behaviour towards you behind closed doors. This would be much harder if the primary source was a friend or colleague.
4. It is from you that we will look to receive some of the shards and segments (further explained below) that are applied to our construct;
5. We will also require a whole range of ancillary benefits which arise from what you are when you are placed in the role of primary source.

Accordingly, the person who becomes our primary source is the most important selection of all those that we interact with. You are our chief provider of fuel and you must give us a whole host of other benefits. We must ensure we make an excellent choice when we choose the person who is to fulfil the role of primary source.

The Supplementary Sources

The supplementary source of fuel is all those who provide us with fuel who fall outside of the primary source. Since the primary source is almost without exception an intimate partner this means that supplementary sources are anybody else we interact with, other than this intimate partner. In ascending order of importance to us this includes: -

Remote strangers

Strangers

Minions

Acquaintances

Colleagues

Outer Circle Friends

Inner Circle Friends

Family

We extract fuel from all these different types of relationship. We also acquire shards and segments from them for the purposes of our construct. We apply consideration (although not as much as we do when we target out primary source) to those people who we want to in these various positions to fulfil their role. This selection applies to nearly all of these categories in the following ways: -

1. Their ability to provide us with positive fuel (occasionally negative – see family but almost exclusively positive);
2. Their capacity to provide something else of use to use e.g. their willingness to give us money, carry out work on our behalf, the provision of a place to live where we need a bolthole during a silent treatment and so on;
3. Their ability to provide us with some trait or attribute which is required for our construct.

These are the three things we look for most of all when we are targeting individuals to be admitted (or remain) within the group of supplementary source. Those are the initial considerations. With those in higher- ranking groups the process is also finessed (which will be described below) in order to determine those who will best provide positive fuel, those who will best provide some other benefit and those who will provides us with the best traits for the construct. The forerunners in those categories, which we identify through a number of methods, become those who we admit into those groupings and form one of our supplementary sources of fuel.

Turning to the groupings.

Remote strangers – these are people we connect with through chatrooms, people we do not know in "real life" who we may have somehow friended on

Facebook and now message. The key attribute we look for in people in this category is the provision of attention and someone who is attracted by the mysterious element of now knowing much about us so that this shrouded part of us provides the person with a 'hook' so they keep contacting us.

Strangers – our interaction with strangers is often on a one-off basis and accordingly we do not choose applicable attributes for these people. If they happen to provide us with fuel, we will take it, but they do not provide a meaningful level of fuel and we have no need to expend time and energy in establishing their credentials to fulfil this role owing to the transient nature of it.

Minions – this category includes people who provide us with a service. We may select a worker in a particular coffee shop not because the coffee shop has a delightful ambience, the customer service is fast nor because the coffee tastes great. No, we will choose this person because they always provide us with attention, they want to talk to us and they regularly compliment us.

Acquaintances – these are people we know in terms of name and having repeated interaction with them albeit on an infrequent basis. We choose those people who provide us with attention and admiration. If the acquaintance fails to deliver on that front they are dropped. There are some acquaintances who will provide us with the necessary traits which we require for our shards and in those circumstances we will maintain contact with them even if they do not provide us with fuel. Their value arises from the fact we can purloin form their sporting or academic achievements and coat ourselves in them.

Colleagues – we look for people who admire our work achievements, who are loyal and for want of a better description they are arse lickers around us, providing us with admiring attention in the hope of being granted some form of privilege by us. We also select industrious and diligent individuals form our colleagues who we will fraternise with on the basis of getting them to do the donkey work so we can focus our efforts on obtaining fuel. Higher ups are also included in this category and we will look to engage with them in terms of fuel and also for the purposes of acquiring their achievements and traits for use in our construct.

Outer Circle Friends – these people are again required for the purposes of the provision of admiring fuel, their potential involvement in my coterie and in certain instances they provide use by being the source for items we need for our construct.

Inner Circle Friends – these people provide fuel and in greater doses and of a greater quality, they provide my Lieutenants and therefore I choose those who are easily swayed by my brilliance, those who show slavish devotion to the cult of me and stand in rapt awe of who I am and what I achieve. Occasionally they will also provide traits for use in the construct.

Family – this is the one category which somewhat distinct from the others. In the other categories I decide who I want form the category in terms of admitting them to being a provider of supplementary fuel. I identify a potential target who I determine will make a good outer circle friend. I realise, perhaps because of geographical distance they could not provide me with the level of fuel that say an Inner Circle Friend might and they certainly could not become a primary source of fuel. I recognise however that this person, who I may have met at say the gym, is easily impressed (as I boasted about how much I could bench press he showed his admiration easily) and through careful questioning (more on this below) I established that in terms of work, earnings, status and outlook he ranked beneath me and therefore would value being able to regard me as a friend. I also established, by reason of the fact he has worked at the same place for 16 years that he demonstrates considerable loyalty. Another trait that I require for someone who is to join my stable as a supplementary source. Accordingly, this person is admitted and becomes an inner circle friend. I targeted him and allowed him access. Family is different. They have already been chosen and therefore it is a case of who gets to stay rather than who is admitted. Those family members who will provide positive fuel, can be trusted, exhibit loyalty and also provide shards for the construct are permitted to interact with me as a supplementary source. I may, because I have to have interaction with a person, allow a family member to remain in the supplementary source purely because I can draw negative fuel from them. If I have to interact with them, because of family connections at family events, dinners and such like, I will find a use for them as a supplier of negative fuel. If a family member provides no use to me in the provision of fuel, be it positive or negative, they have no other uses and they do not provide shards for my construct then I will exclude them and freeze them out. I cannot waste time with someone who provides nothing for my ongoing ambitions and machinations. The composition of these groupings does alter, with turnover being higher in the lower-ranked categories. This will be because by the very nature of the category I have only intermittent interaction with the people in the group or because I choose to change them frequently. The higher-ranked groups have a greater degree of stability but they are not rigid. New members will be acquired and those members which have ceased to function and provide us with those things that we require, to the expected level, will be either turned to provide us with negative fuel or expelled and frozen out.

Accordingly, somebody is friends with a narcissist may suddenly find themselves no longer invited to spend time with the narcissist even though they may feel that they have not done anything wrong. That person will have done. They will have most likely stopped providing fuel (since this is the most important) and they may well have ceased to provide a benefit to use of a different type and/or cease to provide for the construct. Thus this person is cast to one side.

Accordingly, the basis on which we target our victims follows an initial sifting process.
1. This is based on what our needs are dependent on the class of narcissist we are; and
2. It depends on the role that we need to be fulfilled and that which we regard the target as best fulfilling.
3. We apply the most effort and consideration to those who we target for the position of primary source since this is extremely important;
4. We apply less effort and consideration to those who are allocated a role within our supplementary sources, since whilst they are of importance it is less than the role of primary source.
5. The manner in which target our victims is then finessed further according to the above.
6. It is an ongoing process and new victims will replace or be added to old ones.
7. Some victims may move between groups, being promoted and demoted as we see fit. Some victims maybe targeted to fulfil one role but prove to be more suited to another instead, an example would be someone who we consider worthwhile as an intimate partner but as part of the targeting we realise that they would not fulfil our requirements to the required level. They still have value and therefore we would make them an Inner or Outer Circle friend. In the opposite direction we may have a colleague who is part of our supplementary source but we recognise that they would make an excellent primary source and we accordingly elevate them to that position, discarding the existing primary source to make way.

Thus you understand the first step that is applicable to why we target you. It is based on what we are and what role we see for you. The next stage to address is a finessing of the above and the provision of greater detail. Linked to what we are we have particular needs and we will identify victims to target who will achieve those needs for us by virtue of their character and traits. Furthermore, there are generic elements which are applicable to all of our victims, especially those who are chosen as primary sources.

3. Why You Are Chosen

In continuing to examine why you are chosen and targeted by us, there are two chief considerations. The first is based on what we are. The type of narcissist we are and therefore what needs arise from that and what is it that we want in those we target? The second consideration which segues with the above is whether you are a primary source or a supplementary source and what attributes you have that will meet and fulfil our needs.

As with everything that governs our existence, it is all about us and what we need. We target you because we see that you will fulfil our needs. The first and foremost is that you will provide us with fuel. You will give us attention fused with emotion, either though act or words. It may be positive or negative so long as achieve fuel from you. If you will not provide us with fuel or your fuel provision will be weak and intermittent you will not be targeted. We need fuel above everything else and accordingly this because the most important consideration when we target somebody. We need to ascertain what their capability and reliability is for providing this essential essence. I will explain in later chapters how we go about ascertaining your suitability but at this juncture you need to understand that is your capacity for providing fuel and fulfilling our prime need which results in us targeting you.

What does this look like then? Why do some narcissists seek out a particular type of victim compared to others? Our targets share several traits in common and then there are others which are of greater attraction dependent on the type of narcissist we are. First, let us consider the traits that we always look for in all our victims.

The Generic Traits

Love Devotee - we require our targets to be committed to the concept of love. You want to find love, experience love, love and be loved. The idea of love is central to your existence and you truly believe that our purpose on this earth is to love others. Not only does this mean loving those around but above all else you believe in the fulfilment that arises from having that one special person who you are committed to, who you will do anything for and who you will make sacrifices for. The existence of love is a reason, to you to exist and therefore you must find it and once located, obtain it and maintain it.

Fuel benefit - you will furnish us with huge amounts of attention when you believe (through our love bombing) that you have found that special person. You will be moved to compliment us and then once you realise that we want to be with you (because we know you will make an excellent primary source) you will continue to praise, admire, flatter and serve us in order to maintain this love. You will shower us with love just in the way we showered you with love bombs when we seduced you.

Residual Benefit – You will do anything for us. You will look after us, working to support us, cleaning and cooking, doing our laundry, laughing at our jokes, supporting us and so on.

The necessity of you being a Love Devotee is a crucial component of the generic traits.

Compassionate – our target must exhibit compassion. This compassion must be mainly for us although we are content for it to be exhibited for other people and objects such as animals.

Fuel Benefit - by showing compassion you will provide us with emotional attention when we are ill, flapping around us to ensure that we are comfortable, checking how we are feeling. When we demonstrate upset (which will be false) anger, annoyance or discontent you will feel sorry for us and therefore this will manifest in your action as you give us attention and say things to show that you have compassion for us.

Residual Benefit – We know we will be looked after if something bad befalls us. Whether it is illness or injury, loss of employment, financial problems, a bereavement or even our football team losing you will look after us and try to make everything all right again.

Decent – We look for decent people. People who are well-mannered, polite and understanding. People who have consideration for others, wait their turn in speaking, allowing others to take a slice of cake before anyone else, giving to charity and conducting him or herself in a dignified manner.

Fuel Benefit - a decent person does not like conflict and therefore when we create conflict you will take steps to extinguish it by giving us attention. You may seek to soothe us or express anger towards us but either way it is providing us with fuel and therefore is what we want.

Residual Benefit - you will invariably behave in a decent manner towards us but more importantly you will be well-regarded by others (at least so long as we allow this). This makes you a trophy primary source for us and will also provide an additional flow of fuel. People will congratulate us on having such a well-mannered, polite and decent primary source, I mean intimate partner on our arm.

Moral Compass - we prefer a person with a strong moral compass, somebody who would hand a wallet to the police with the contents intact if they found such an item in the street or they would alert the shop assistant if they were handed too much change. This person is monogamous and faithful and believes others should conduct themselves by a similar moral code.

Fuel Benefit – a person who has a strong moral compass becomes outraged by our behaviour during devaluation since it contravenes the code by which they live. This causes them to react in a heightened emotional fashion and provide us with fuel. It also means that they will try very hard to make us see the error of our ways which provides further fuel as they first do so in a concerned manner and then become frustrated. This person is more likely to remain in the relationship and stay as a primary source of fuel by trying to repair our damaged selves.

Residual Benefit – this person draws praise for the way that they conduct themselves and this reflects well on us for having allowed them to be our intimate partner. They are also loyal and faithful to us.

Caring – an individual who will always look after somebody else. Whether it is through working to provide for us, running the home in an excellent manner, looking after us when we are ill and being concerned about our well-being, the caring trait is very important and must be evident in our primary source especially.

Fuel Benefit – by being concerned about us they will flow with positive fuel during seduction and when they are subjected to devaluation they will still continue to care, usually becoming upset and hurt rather than angry when we subject this person to such manipulations as a silent treatment or intimidation. They will want to make sure everything is alright and will work hard to achieve this, pouring out their emotion and providing us with fuel.

Residual Benefit – we are well looked-after by this domestic goddess. Our meals are cooked, our laundry is taken care of, the house is tidy, we have a nurse when we are ill and someone who dotes on us.

Honest – a person who tells the truth although will not do so in a blunt or sanctimonious fashion. He or she will not lie, will not engage in deceit and cannot hide how they feel about people or a situation.

Fuel Benefit – this person will also give an honest reaction to our seduction where they will gush with delight and our devaluation where they will be hurt, upset and angry. They cannot mask the way they feel, cloak it or disguise it and as a consequence they provide fuel most readily.

Residual Benefit - the honest individual will never do anything which could compromise us through deceit, for example stealing our money or possessions, even when subjected to devaluation.

Need to Understand – empathic individuals always need to understand why something has happened. They want to know how and why someone has reacted the way they have or said the things that have been said. Their desire to understand is linked to their desire to help and place themselves in the shoes of someone else. Empathic individuals hate not knowing why something is as it is.

Fuel Benefit - this trait means that the individual will persevere with trying to establish why we have behaved in a certain way. This refusal to give up and just accept it is as it is means they will become upset and frustrated and consequently provide us with fuel. Their need to understand makes them especially attentive as they try to get us to explain why we have acted in a certain way.

Residual Benefit – this individual will remain with us rather than walk away as they try to figure us out, work out what is happening and find a solution (although of course they never can because they are approaching the position from their world view point and not ours, thus what we do will never make sense to them). This indefatigable spirit causes this person to be susceptible to our manipulations such as circular conversations, as they will not let go.

Support the Underdog – this person allows helps the less advantaged individual, they stand up for the weak, the bullied and the dispossessed and see it as a natural role for themselves in doing this.
Fuel Benefit – this individual hangs in there when they are being pressed and intimidated. Their response is likely to be fiery and angry which provides us with fuel. They will battle on, trying to win a fight even though they cannot and in doing so they continue to provide us with fuel as the try and fight back.
Residual Benefit – this person is tenacious and should we hail from the cadre of Victim Narcissist they will always fight out corner which we revel in as they will engage with people on our behalf to help us out, thus saving us energy and aggravation.

Strives for the Truth – this person must get to the bottom of everything and find out what the truth of the matter is. They are not easily dissuaded, they hate being lied to and want those who they engage with to always tell them the truth.
Fuel Benefit – this person reacts emotionally when they realise they are being lied to. Since we lie all the time it is like pouring fuel on a fire and they will also respond to these lies in an emotional fashion and thus provide fuel. They will also not back down as they try to get us to tell the truth. We know

this and will continue to frustrate their efforts so they continue to provide us with fuel.

Residual Benefit – such an individual who strives for the truth is unlikely to let go and consequently we know they will remain bound to us for some considerable time.

Excellent Listener – we do not want someone who will not listen to us because words, more so than actions, are our weapons. We want someone who will sit and listen to our monologues and then lavish us with praise and admiration, we want someone who will listen to us even when we are upbraiding and lashing out at them, rather than someone who will retreat from us. Thus it is important for us to find that person who is an excellent listener

Fuel Benefit – this person remains listening to monologue or tirade and will provide a reaction to it and thus provide us with fuel.

Residual Benefit – this individual will remain with us as they cannot bear not to hear what is being said, even if it is unpleasant. Accordingly, we can rely on their loyalty for some time.

These are the attributes which are present in all those who we target for the position of primary source. We look for these in people when we wish to establish a primary source and as I will describe below we have a variety of ways of establishing whether these attributes are present or not in a person. We need to ensure that a target has these traits because they are the fundamental drivers behind the provision of fuel. They also provide residual benefits to us.

Next come what I refer to as the Class Traits which are those traits which are either evident in some of our targets and not others, or the trait is particularly strong and prevalent in a target and therefore that individual will attract a particular class of narcissist.

Class Traits

The Lesser or Mid-Range Victim Narcissist

The LVN or MRVN will look for the following traits in his or victims when targeting him or her.

- Physically weaker than the narcissist. This is because this type of narcissist often resorts to physical violence in order to manipulate and therefore will not want a target which could fight back or even worse overpower the narcissist. Like any bully, this type of narcissist wants someone smaller, lighter and weaker than him or her.
- A consummate care giver. The caring element for this target must be higher than usual since they are expected to undertake a role of looking after the narcissist across every level. Refer back to the description of the Victim Narcissist above for more information on how he or she requires being cared for in terms of health, shelter, food, money and so forth.
- The target must not be swayed by looks or physical prowess. If they are they will not be seduced to the necessary degree by this narcissist and/or be at risk of going elsewhere since this narcissist will not score highly in terms of attractiveness and/or physical prowess. A square-jawed muscle man or curvaceous siren they are not.
- The target must not be swayed by intelligence or academic ability for reasons similar to the paragraph above
- A bleeding heart. The target is being "seduced" by a fairly unattractive prospect (at least judged by ordinary standards) and

therefore it is necessary for the target to have excessive degrees of sympathetic for the down trodden and down at heel.

- A mothering character. The target loves nothing more than replicating that unconditional and never-ending love and care that a normal mother provides.
- The target is unlikely to be a high-achiever in looks, employment, career, intellect and such like. Whilst they will be far from at the bottom end of those categories (since they need to be able to provide for this type of narcissist) the narcissist does not want a high-achiever who is beautiful and capable as there is a risk that they will fail to be seduced by this narcissist or they will look elsewhere during the relationship and abandon the narcissist. The narcissist will be aiming low (but not as low as him or her) on these categories.
- The target is not swayed by money or the status of their partner. These factors are not important.
- The target has little interest in their caring being reciprocated, for them the act of loving and caring provides them with sufficient fulfilment of their role in life, they need not be defined by love being returned or by praise for what they do. If that is shown they regard it as a bonus.
- A low sex drive but not non-existent. The victim narcissist only uses sex in order to draw sympathy. A target with a higher sex drive may be prone to abandon this type on narcissist.
- The target must exhibit a particular desire to care and nurture as one might with a child.
- Companionship is valued by the target since this type of narcissist will often be at home (lack of employment, not socially dynamic) or even housebound (injury or illness)

- This narcissist is not interested in someone who is stimulating, entertaining or a social butterfly. Those traits are regarded as dangerous by this narcissist
- The target should not have interests outside of the narcissist and running the home, other than earning an income. The narcissist not only requires the target to be focussed on him but he also does not want someone who may abandon him for better prospects.
- If the target already has children this is regarded as a positive since it demonstrates a maternal and caring approach by the narcissist. The narcissist will also look to ensure the target is soon pregnant as this will be regarded as a key method of binding the target to the narcissist so he or she remains to care for both the narcissist and his offspring.

The Victim Narcissist gains fuel from having someone attend to him or her, principally in the role as a glorified care giver. The "clucking" around the narcissist will provide him or her with positive fuel. Once this narcissist starts devaluation he will aim his manipulations at undermining the caring competency of his victim in order to strike at the central trait of his victim. This will wound the most and draw the more heightened emotional responses. There are many residual benefits arising for this type of narcissist who is essentially provided for on many levels.

Mid-Range and Greater Cerebral Narcissist

The MRCN and the GCN look for the following traits when targeting their victims: -

- An appreciation of knowledge
- An interest in the wider world i.e. they are not content to sit and watch soaps on television
- Intellectual capability but not to the standard of this narcissist
- An interest in discussion, debate, reading, current affairs, religion and politics. Such traits mean that the target will engage with the narcissist on these topics and in so doing will provide a platform for this type of narcissist to exhibit his superiority and show off
- A particularly good and attentive listener since this type of narcissist is prone to embark on major monologues but will expect the target to paying attention
- An interest in the acquisition of knowledge
- An interest in academia, studying for qualifications and similar achievements
- A keen interest in music (both playing and listening)
- Appreciative of plays, films, art but again not to the standard of this narcissist and content to be lectured to by the narcissist
- The physical appearance of the target is not of great concern although this narcissist will avoid a target that is notable physical superior (strong/athletic) to avoid the risk of the target fighting back during devaluation

- Sociable
- Exhibits caring but this narcissist is more concerned with those who will be wowed and who will admire. He or she wants a target that will provide him or her with a platform from which the narcissist can show off
- Compliant individual who will instigate discussion and debate to allow the narcissist to hijack the discussion and demonstrate his innate superiority

The fuel this type of narcissist receives is all based on the admiration he receives from the primary source. There is the residual benefit which arises from the fact that other people will admire the fact that the narcissist has an intelligent, conversant and interesting primary source. The narcissist will take delight in touting the primary source around to use as a sounding board for his own excellence and a method of exhibiting his intellectual superiority.

The Mid-Range and Greater Somatic Narcissist

The MRSN or GSN will look for the following traits and attributes in his or her victims.

- Athletic and in decent physical condition to allow the target to participate in sports and outdoor physical pursuits with the narcissist
- High sex drive. The sexual arena is the exhibition stand for the somatic narcissist. It is where he or she gathers a lot of fuel and also plies their manipulative practices on the target. Accordingly, they will want someone who will engage with them in this arena.

- No real in interest in the arts, books, reading, playing music. Although the target may have an interest in these things to a degree (and doing so will not necessarily put the narcissist off) the somatic narcissist prefers the level of interest to be low or non-existent so that these more intellectual pursuits do not get in the way of pursuing those activities which are best suited to allow the somatic narcissist to showcase his or her talents. Furthermore, the somatic narcissist will not want someone whose attention is focussed on something that he is not engaged in nor will he or she want as a primary source somebody who is likely to show superiority in certain fields to him or her as this will offend the narcissist and result in limited fuel prospects.
- A sociable and outgoing nature, albeit not beyond the narcissist's own level of sociability and affability. The somatic narcissist loves to be seen. Like a strutting peacock she or he wants to be admired in terms of how her or she looks, their physique, their clothing and the environment in which they are witnessed. Accordingly, they will look for a target who enjoys going out and will facilitate and complement this narcissist's need for such attention.
- Fashionable and interested in taking care of their appearance. This is again to complement the narcissist but not outshine him or her.
- Interested in shopping, home improvements, appliances. These are the status symbols which matter to the narcissist. Not only will he want to be seen strolling around the shopping mall looking magnificent, he will want to ensure that he is seen purchasing a pair of expensive shoes or trying on the latest style of suit. Appliances which are of the moment and attractive also appeal to this narcissist and therefore they will want to acquire a target which has a similar level of interest.
- Holidays and travel. Again this provides for another showcasing environment for this narcissist. Whether it is taking selfies having walked to the top of a mountain or showing off his tanned and toned body on a beach, this narcissist will want somebody who will accompany him and

enhance his showing off. This narcissist would never contemplate holidaying alone.
- Interested in healthy living from diets to exercise to beauty products. The narcissist here will want to share these interests in order to allow him to show off but also to have a helper who will wax his back, make his protein shakes and so forth.
- The target must take pride in their appearance. They must never eclipse this narcissist but since they are very much regarded as a trophy they must still look good
- Be physically attractive. This narcissist wants to be reminded of how attractive he or she is by looking on somebody who is also attractive.
- This narcissist will want somebody who is interested in having children with him or her as this is a golden opportunity to create beautiful and handsome offspring in their own image, allowing their showcasing to continue through their children.

The Mid-Range or Greater Elite Narcissist

The MREN or GEN will look for a target which exhibits the applicable traits which prove attractive to both somatic and cerebral narcissists so long as those attributes do not outshine the narcissist. We will want someone who is attractive but also shows an interest in politics for example. They are our trophy on two fronts; both in the physical sense and the intellectual sense. Since the elite narcissist combines the traits of both the somatic and cerebral narcissist he or she is also attracted by the applicable traits for both these classes of narcissist. Whereas a cerebral narcissist is not interested in and does not want a target that is of a greater physical presence than him, the elite narcissist wants the target to be attractive and have some physical prowess to allow him or her to complement our need to exhibit our physical attributes such as hill walking or attending the gym. The important factor is to ensure that the target will not outshine us in any particular trait. The MREN or GEN will also look for these additional traits: -

- Leaders in their field. This is applicable to those targets who are selected to form part of the supplementary sources. A leader in their field is unlikely to be a primary source because the narcissist will not risk being eclipsed. This is not a concern where the individual has been ear marked as a supplementary source. In such an instance this individual will provide the narcissist with reflected glory and also character traits which the narcissist can acquire as part of the construct. Elite narcissists are more likely to have the ability to fraternise with leaders in their field, compared to other classes of narcissist because their level of charm combined with their physical presence and intellectual ability allows them a greater chance of accessing and interacting with the leaders in their fields.
- Large audiences. Not a trait as such but especially in terms of supplementary sources of fuel the elite narcissist enjoys the presence of an audience more than other classes of narcissist and therefore is prone to seeking out such platforms by which an audience can be acquired.
- Humour. Elite narcissists exhibit the best sense of humour out of all classes of narcissist. The Victim Narcissist is too busy complaining about his ailments, the Somatic Narcissist may engage in physical humour – pranks and slapstick behaviour and the Cerebral Narcissist applies sarcasm and dry wit but in terms of the best form of humour and most accessible it comes from the elite narcissist. Accordingly, we will look for a good sense of humour to appreciate our excellent sense of humour in our targets.
- Challenging individuals. Being of a superior class means that we can tackle those targets which are more challenging. A classic example is that an elite narcissist will seek targets who have borderline personality disorder. The

Victim Narcissist will not find the level of mothering required from someone with BPD. The somatic narcissist may find some attraction to a promiscuous BPD target but will not be attracted by their capacity to seek out attention from other people through that promiscuity. The cerebral narcissist will regard a BPD target as too much like hard work even though there is plenty of fuel available and will hold the BPD target in contempt. The elite narcissist will relish the chance to bring a BPD target under his wind and exert his control. The drama which surrounds a BPD target owing to their emotionally thin skin proves highly attractive to the elite narcissist and owing to his superior abilities he is able to handle the less desirable elements of the BPD target such as neediness. The target need not be personality disordered but be of strong character and independent. This proves a challenge to the elite narcissist who will relish breaking these traits and then showing the world how fearsome he is as he drinks deep of the fuel that flows from breaking such an individual. Accordingly, independent, strong-willed and disciplined empathic individuals will prove attractive targets to us.

- Gold-diggers. The elite narcissist is entirely comfortable with targeting the gold digger as he or she will trade their attentiveness to us in exchange for being furnished with the trappings of success and money. We know that that for all the largesse they enjoy they will earn every penny in terms of supplying us with fuel. Indeed, their desire to maintain that lifestyle and not lose it, once they have experienced it, will cause them to be bound to us. Hangers-on will be welcomed by all narcissists but especially the elite narcissist who will place them in the category of supplementary source whilst allowing them to reap some of the benefits of our elevated status whilst ensuring they more than contribute through the provision of fuel.

All classes of narcissist will be looking to recruit to their ranks of supplementary sources and also picking that prize candidate for the role of primary source. The traits above are applicable to all potential targets of the particular narcissist. Where the primary source is being recruited then the relevant narcissist will look for as many traits as possible which accord with his own needs to ensure that the person selected as primary source discharges their role as the prime supplier of fuel in the most effective manner possible.

Those who are identified as supplementary sources need not fit all the required traits but should sit within the relevant parameters for the class of narcissist. For example, a Cerebral Narcissist will want those who supply supplemental fuel to be say members of his book group, or a friends who are interested in bell-ringing. He will not want to recruit them from a group of football fans or those who belong to a cycling club. When recruiting we ascertain whether you should be considered as a supplemental source or whether you will make the grade as a primary source and our method of seduction will be tailored accordingly. Naturally the primary source target will be the recipient of a sustained and potent love bombing campaign. Where we identify an individual who will provide us with heightened emotional response and thus more fuel they will always be considered as a primary source unless there is an overriding reason why this is not appropriate (e.g. wrong sex for a relationship).

In addition to the generic traits and the class traits there are additional factors that we will look for which are the special traits. These are generally speaking the preserve of those we target as primary sources.

The Special Traits

Gullibility - most people when first dealing with other people take that person at face value. If that person explains they are a teacher in a secondary school, then the listener will accept that to be the case until some glaring contradiction appears. Most listeners will not immediately challenge the speaker's assertion that he or she is a teacher. The listener will not ask questions in order to elicit information from the speaker which corroborates that assertion. Some cynical and suspicious people may behave in this manner but the majority will not. This acceptance of what is stated is the default setting. There are however those who readily accept and moreover delight in what they are being told and do not think to question it. Those gullible individuals are treasured by us as they are even easier than usual to seduce. They are readily taken in by what we tell them and continue to always believe that we say.

Pleasers - these individuals are almost masochistic in the way that they want other people to be happy before they are. Indeed, they place the happiness and contentment above their own needs, maintaining that their fulfilment arises from ensuring that others are content and provided for. This type of person will always ensure everyone else has a generous portion of dinner even if this means a smaller amount for him or her. They will accede to someone else's preference to a night out over their own. They will endure discomfort if it means that someone else is happier and better off. It is akin to the unconditional love that a parent provides to a child but of course these people behave in such a manner to adults. Such an individual who is a pleaser will provide us with more fuel and will endure a harsher devaluation but still remain in situ compared to those who are not pleasers.

Susceptibility to manipulation – our manipulative behaviours which I have detailed in **Manipulated** and **The Devil's Toolkit** are difficult to resist but there are certain people who are easily manipulated as a consequence of their lack of self-esteem and diminished confidence. These people are attractive to us because we can expend less energy in applying our manipulations against them, they are less likely to resist them and we will be able to move them into a state of dependency in a shorter time period.

Damaged – damaged people are those who have some significant vulnerability which means that not only are they easier to seduce and abuse, but they actively find themselves drawn to our kind. Owing to whatever damage they have suffered they will look to us as their saviour and cling to us no matter what. Those who have been hitherto starved of love and affection, those who have been bullied, socially ostracised, prejudiced against and victimised are damaged and they show up as a bright light on our radar. Often they may not even realise that their compulsion to be with us arises from their damaged state, since it may be subtle yet powerful. Those who fear abandonment, excessively crave love and especially those who are the victims of our kind previously (a narcissistic parent or former intimate partner being the most effective methods of tenderising and damaging this individual) attract considerable interest from our kind. By way of example, if I am assessing a target and she admits to me that she has "daddy issues" then a green light immediately switches on to confirm that she is damaged and therefore has one of the special traits.

It is worth a passing mention in respect of the type of people we will not target. We do not tend to target another narcissist. We recognise one another, most of the time, and know that the prospects for fuel are limited and therefore we avoid targeting. Cynical people are left alone as they will question too much and are unlikely to succumb to our charm offensive or require far too much effort for a limited gain of fuel. The self-obsessed are avoided too since they fail to exhibit the traits we require as they are caught up in their own lives and whilst they may not be one of our kind they certainly exhibit similar qualities, albeit it on a lesser scale. Indeed, the more narcissistic qualities an individual demonstrates, even if they would not qualify as one of us, the less appealing they are, certainly in terms of a primary source. We may engage with such individuals infrequently purely in order to gather traits and shards for our construct but we know not to rely on them for fuel.

Our targets are drawn from the following groups of people since they exhibit the generic, class and special traits in varying degrees.

Normal – the majority of people in the world. They do not possess much by way of narcissistic traits so they are not unappealing but they also score low in terms of empathic traits and therefore are only really suitable as supplementary sources of fuel. Most normal people are "good". They have no desire to hurt anyone else, they do not want to be hurt, they show some degree of care-giving and interest in other people but they also recognise they need to look out for themselves as well. They put themselves first over others but not to the extent of trampling on other people or parking their tanks on the lawns of others. These people want to be able to get on with their lives without complication. Neither being burdened by the machinations of our kind nor by having to care in an excessive and sacrificial manner. In essence, they want the quiet life. These are the people who readily accept the façade, do not want to rock the boat or cause a scene. They react to the presence of greatness, superiority and charm in a favourable manner but they feel no pressing need to be tightly bound to our kind. Their relative position of neutrality between our kind and the empathic (although they lean more to the empathic than to us) means that they are ideal for being recruited to the supplementary source category.

The Empath – exhibiting the generic traits and numerous class traits, this individual seeks to help and heal through their devotion to love, ability to step into the shoes of others and their kindness to other people. There may be the existence of special traits as well. The empath is recruited for both primary and supplementary sources, but is always considered for the position of primary source. If this is occupied, they will be prepared in readiness for replacement once the existing primary source is discarded. They will also be slotted into supplementary positions if the primary source (both existing and proposed) positions are occupied. We can never have too many empathic souls in our grasp.

The Super-Empath – empath 2.0. Possessing more of the special traits, oozing with empathic qualities and a regular martyr, the super empath will always put us before themselves and they behave in a masochistic way, deriving pleasure from seeing our needs met ahead of their own. This individual will always be snapped up as a primary source and should one venture into our sights when we have an existing primary source already, the super empath will be ensnared and the existing primary source jettisoned, such is their value. A veritable super tanker of fuel.

The Co-Dependent – this is a super empath who chains themselves to us because they are dependent on us for their existence until such time as they receive outside help to escape what they are and our fierce grip on them. The gift that always keeps on giving, the co-dependent is highly prized, is always a primary source and is only discarded for a short period before easily being Hoovered again, such is their value to us. My book **Chained** goes into more detail about the Co-dependent. If you recognise that you are one, you need us and we want you more than anyone else. You will have our kind fighting it out to secure your fuel and is one of the few occasions where you may witness a narcissist becoming undone at the hands of another such is the ferocity by which we behave in order to ensnare the co-dependent.

Accordingly, you need to understand which type of narcissist you have been involved with and therefore are likely to attract. You know the generic traits which all our targets will have, the specific class traits that are applicable and attract different classes of narcissist and we also look for those who possess the special traits also. In our assessment of you as we target you, we will consider whether you will suffice as a supplementary source of fuel or whether you should be upgraded and targeted as a primary source instead. You know the categories of victim we look for and who proves the most attractive to us. This classification is based on how many and how strongly you comply with the traits we seek. I shall detail in a later chapter how we identify these traits as we target you, but next we shall consider where my kind carry out their targeting. It is time to visit the hunting grounds.

4. The Hunting Grounds

Our kind will find our victims anywhere and everywhere. We have no qualms about gathering fuel from those we target in any circumstance or environment. The need for fuel is paramount and as a consequence when an opportunity presents itself to acquire fuel, no matter how small or large, we will naturally take it. This means that all situations are ones whereby our kind will look for fuel. It is usually by reference to a supplemental source in the general environment since the prospects of finding a succulent primary source are slimmer (although not non-existent). Since we are creatures of economy not only do we target certain people but we target certain environments to ensure that we stand a better chance of securing improved supplementary sources and most of all a better chance of ensnaring a suitable primary source of fuel. Certain classes of narcissist operate in specific hunting grounds since their type of target will be more prevalent. By contrast, certain classes of narcissist will rarely be seen in certain environments as their prospects of securing a suitable primary source will be virtually nil and even the opportunity to obtain supplementary sources of fuel will be much diminished. Accordingly, in order to secure our fuel, we choose our hunting grounds carefully. Knowing which class of narcissist you attract and where they may be lurking will allow you to determine whether there are places you are better off avoiding or at the very least you can ensure that your narc radar is tuned, turned up and fully functioning when you venture into these places. I will detail the various hunting grounds and which class of narcissist is going to be found there in a table form to begin with and then provide expanded commentary below.

Type of Establishment	Attended by which Ns	Preferred by
Bar	All	All
Restaurant	All	V, C and E
Nightclubs	S and E	S
Academic	C, V and E	C
Hospital/Doctors	V, C and E	V and C
Bank	S, C and E	E
Office	C, S and E	E
Concerts	S	S
Libraries	C and E	C
Sporting Events	S and E	S
Debating Society	C and E	C
Museums	C and E	C
Arts and Crafts Clubs	V	None
Outdoor Pursuits	S and E	S
Shopping Mall	S	S
Neighbourhood	S, V and E	E
Charity Organisations	E and V	V
Swimming	S and E	S
Gym	S and E	S
Swinging venues	S and E	S
Social Media	All	C and V
Dating Sites	All	All

Bars - all types of narcissists will frequent bars because these are regarded as social hubs where there will be repeated and different opportunities to target people. The Victim Narcissist will be found sat in the corner, often alone, or drinking at the bar in a quiet establishment. He will hope to attract the interest of a suitably mothering individual. It is a quality of empaths that you like to talk to strangers because you like to learn about people and get to know them in order to better understand life. Accordingly, the Victim narcissist will be content to wait in the hope of being detected by an appropriately mothering empath. He will also rely on frequenting the same bar so that he is known to and liked by the staff there with the possibility of attracting their attention and drawing their empathic sympathy and interest. The Cerebral Narcissist is not averse to using a bar to target his victims, especially if for example it is situated on a university campus or next to a theatre. The patrons will therefore exhibit sapiosexuality and prime targets for the cerebral narcissist. He will prefer quieter bars where he can be heard and will often use his coterie as sounding boards for his intellect in order to impress a potential target who is nearby. The somatic narcissist is a keen attendee of a bar, especially those which are regarded as trendy, are loud and busy. He does not need to do much talking but instead takes up a central position or in the VIP section where he is on display, showing his peacock feathers and thus attracting attention. He relies on his looks and overall appearance to land the first blow, drawing in a prospective target and once he has acquired their interest he will be pushing on an open door. We of the elite variety are entirely comfortable in any type of bar being able to adapt ourselves to suit the environment in pursuit of fuel.

Restaurants - expect to find the Victim Narcissist at fast-food joints, roadside diners and greasy spoons. The fare is no nonsense like him and he will, as in the pub scenario be a committed regular looking to gradually attract the attention of either staff or another regular patron. He will use his charm on those who serve him, especially those who cook, recognising the value of having someone who exhibits culinary skill in order to provide for him. The Cerebral Narcissist will attend readily high-end restaurants where he is able to opine to his assembled coterie about the wine, the origin of the food and all manner of cuisine related observations. The Cerebral Narcissist is likely to be a member of a dining club which will expose him to like-minded individuals who take an interest in tasting their food rather than just wolfing it down. The Somatic Narcissist will attend restaurants on the basis of the status attached to being seen there and the prospect of finding like-minded social climbers. He is not especially interested in the dining experience however as this necessitates a lot of conversation when he would much rather be demonstrating his physical superiority which is somewhat hampered by being sat down. The Somatic Narcissist will not choose a restaurant as a primary hunting ground.

Nightclubs – such an environment is not for the Victim Narcissist. It is too loud and chaotic for him and his various limitations will be exposed. Given the nature of those who attend nightclubs he is unlikely to find anybody feeling sorry for him here and will instead be most likely to be subjected to ridicule which will wound him with little recourse to gathering fuel, accordingly he will not be found here. Similarly, the Cerebral Narcissist will be negated by the noise and therefore his main method of seduction, his oration will be nullified. It is an early night instead for him. The Elite Narcissist will be at ease here but it is not his or her preferred venue. It is here that the Somatic Narcissist rules the roost. The nightclub environment is the preserve of the beautiful and hip and he will be moving amongst these delightful creatures wowing them with his looks, attire and moreover his dancing. The Somatic Narcissist will be found in the centre of the dance floor with a circle of admirers surrounding him as he puts on a display worthy of Saturday Night Fever. The ready prevalence of targets who have also been drinking for some time, the existence of VIP areas and the heady mix of light, noise and expectant sexual congress means this is a fertile environment for the Somatic Narcissist. The lateness of the hour also allows him the opportunity to lure his target to his home or to impose himself on theirs and extend the targets period of exposure to his assessment and likely seduction.

Academic Institutions – this covers schools through to colleges and universities. The Somatic Narcissist will not be here; he will still be locked together with last night's target as the eager Cerebral Narcissist makes a bee line for the environment where he has plenty of low-hanging fruit. Able to shine with his intellect, garner shards from other academics and find those who are attracted to the power of the mind, the Cerebral Narcissist stalks such institutions on a regular basis. A Cerebral Narcissist may take a position in a school (usually seeking Deputy Head of Head, Vice Principal or Principal, well after all he must be looked up to) but the preponderance of educators who are there to educate but also nurture provides numerous opportunities to target appropriate victims amongst the teaching staff. In Higher and Further Education, the Cerebral Narcissist is even more at home amidst the more esteemed academic minds and he will have thousands of potential targets from both staff and students when at university. The opportunity to charm an undergraduate with his impressive intellect is too great an opportunity to pass up. The Cerebral Narcissist may belong to the student body, either as an undergraduate, post graduate or a mature student. He may take up night classes which allow him to dip into another pool of potential targets. The Elite Narcissist will also make use of these places although he will prefer to secure positions of authority at these institutions in order to exhibit his superiority when leaning to his cerebral side. The political game playing that often exists in higher education will also appeal to his Machiavellian nature allowing him to acquire significant supplementary fuel sources by manipulating the staff around him and toying with the students he has in his tutorial group. Whereas the Cerebral Narcissist will use the environment to secure his fuel and exhibit his brilliance, the Greater Elite Narcissist will regard it as a place to find fuel but also to game play. The large egos that will prevail in such a place will prove irresistible to him as he looks to lure them to him and then provoke negative reactions. There is even a place for the Victim Narcissist. He may sign up for improvement courses and adult learning. He has no desire to learn anything or even see out the course but he will be searching for a favourable reaction from the course provider or possibly other members of the course who will take pity on his clumsy attempts at Spanish or ham-fisted culinary endeavours. The Victim Narcissist is unlikely to use this environment in an employment sense since he has little interest in work and he would only be able to secure menial work such as care-taking and labouring which would leave him largely invisible to the majority of those who operate in an academic institutional environment.

Hospital/Doctors - The Somatic Narcissist is absent from this environment. Places where the injured and the sick are plentiful means that it is anathema to him. You may think that he would welcome the opportunity to show just how far removed he is from the infirm and diseased by showing off his radiant health but the distaste he experiences far outweighs any benefit he might receive. Moreover, the Somatic Narcissist would be most likely despised and envied for flaunting his vitality and whilst this would provide him with negative fuel it would be of no use to him in finding a primary source since he needs that target to want him and desire him.

The Cerebral Narcissist will be found in a medical role allowing him to demonstrate that he is God by determining the illnesses of those attending the consulting room or accident and emergency but by dispensing healing and remedies form his vast and encyclopaedic knowledge of all matters health related. He will stroll along the wards a behemoth with a coterie of junior doctors following behind him listening in rapt attention to his theories and diagnoses. He will lap up the grateful praise of patients and the admiring glances of the nurses but he will only of course feign a caring attitude. His bedside manner is carefully constructed but as soon as he leaves the ward his contempt for the sick and injured soon manifests and he cannot wait to escape them and return to his research. The Cerebral Narcissist is able to draw fuel from so many people, colleagues, patients, family members of patients and support staff. A Mid-Range Cerebral Narcissist may even adopt a fraudulent position within a medical setting, especially if a particular position has been wrongly denied to him. Using his innate ability and also significant powers of mimicry he can easily pose as a doctor in a different discipline or a consultant in his own and ensnare a primary source and gather much by way of supplementary sources.

The Victim Narcissist will be a frequent malingering presence in the consulting room of his general practitioner doctor. If he cannot secure an appointment, he will attend accident and emergency although neither is applicable to his situation. He will feign injuries and illnesses in order to gain fuel from supplementary sources and in the hope of ensnaring a member of the nursing staff to become his intimate partner and thus his primary source. The Victim Narcissist will often make appointments with dentists, opticians and such like in order to keep his supplementary fuel source topped up and he will move between various GP practices, walk-in centres, day-care centres and so forth in order to maintain this fuel but also to find this primary source. Those in this most caring of profession are targeted significantly by the Victim Narcissist as they seek to create a bond between them and a professional caregiver. Whilst the Cerebral Narcissist revels in flexing his intellectual muscle, the Greater Elite Narcissist does so also but he also uses this environment to carry out schemes to draw negative fuel by denigrating colleagues for incompetence, admonishing patients for malingering and upbraiding administrators and support staff for failing to carry out their roles properly in supporting his glorious empire. The nature of a medical environment is such that life and death regularly dance around one another, severe illness and life-changing injuries means that the air is cracking with emotion. From saving a life and the tear-stained gratitude of the relatives to the delivery of a fatal prognosis with sanctimonious declarations of "we did all we can" the matrix of emotional responses provides a fertile hunting ground for these narcissists. If you are a patient, care provider, medic or similar you will have narcissists moving in your midst. The medical environment is too potent to be ignored.

Banking/Finance - the Victim Narcissist being a creature of poverty, poor career prospects and limited income capability will steer clear of such an environment. Instead, his brother narcissists stalk this environment. The Cerebral Narcissist embraces it as the world of derivatives, bonds and complex transactions appeals to him and allows him to shine. The Somatic Narcissist is drawn to it purely by the fact that it involves money and his love of money means he cannot miss an opportunity to show off. He will rely more on brazen charm, chutzpah and a thick skin to allow him to take his barrow boy background and apply it in the trading pit. Money is sexy and he is all about sexy. The testosterone driven atmosphere of trading rooms appeals both to the Somatic and the Elite Narcissist. There are huge opportunities to gather supplementary sources here from admiring colleagues as audacious trades are made using other people's money. There is plenty of scope as well for gathering shards since financiers and investors rub shoulders with the traders and investment bankers. There may be limited scope for the acquisition of primary sources in this environment as the female gender is under represented in what is still a male dominated world in investment banking but that only encourages the Elite Narcissist as ensnaring an acolyte and rubbing his competitors' noses in the dirt provides him with the kind of challenge which generates considerable fuel.

Even in the comparatively sedate world of retail and personal banking there are many opportunities to ensnare both primary and supplementary sources. Repeated visits with the bank manager provides a narcissist holding that position (and the power of decision making over someone's business staying afloat or personal overdraft being extended) means that there is plenty of opportunity for identifying targets. Detailed knowledge of customers' financial positions will allow our kind to exploit certain vulnerabilities or strengths to our advantage. The financial sector will attract narcissists given the nature of the subject matter, the power that is attached to money matters and the willing supplicants that will be found in that environment also. The Elite Narcissist is best suited to the environment in order to target prospective fuel sources as he is able to combine the intellectual rigour required with the personal touch.

The Office - Once again the Victim Narcissist will be missing. The other three cadres of narcissist all utilise the office as a useful hunting ground. The advantage for the narcissist is that there is a high proportion of office workers thus increasing the amount of supplementary fuel to be gained. There is less likelihood of finding a quality primary source and whilst they exist, the narcissist may well adopt a position of using the office environment for gathering plenty of supplementary fuel and going to other hunting grounds for the primary source. Underlings, secretaries, juniors and so on provide a veritable battery of fuel sources and the higher ups provide the opportunity for us to collect some traits for our construct. As you would expect, The Cerebral Narcissist uses his intellect to wow his admirers, the Somatic Narcissist relies on his looks and sheer physical presence to win people over irrespective of his role. The Somatic narcissist of the three is most likely to seek his primary source elsewhere, say in a running club at the weekend or at the gym. The Elite Narcissist fares the best, combining the best of both worlds which provides him with a particular advantage in gathering fuel. The Greater variety also revels in the fuel opportunities which arise from the endless opportunities to play office politics, frustrating promotions, spreading rumours, dumping work on underlings, elevating his coterie beyond their ability and so on.

The hunting ground of the office should not be underestimated in its opportunities to provide a significant volume of fuel for us.

Concerts - It is only the Somatic Narcissist who hunts here. The Victim Narcissist finds the noise and activity too much and has no chance of gaining fuel. The Cerebral Narcissist would rarely attend a pop or rock concert. Even though a classical concert may appeal to him he would find little fuel there as he would not be able to hold forth during the performance. He may before and after but that potential gains are not worth the energy expenditure. Similarly, the Elite Narcissist is hindered by the absence of being able to make himself heard and he won't quite have the full advantage enjoyed by the Somatic Narcissist. The Somatic Narcissist will exploit the opportunity to show off in front of the crowd, he will look great, dance away at rock or pop concert and ensure he is seen. He will occupy himself taking selfies to send to waiting admirers during the concert and like a lead singer scouring the audience for willing groupies, the Somatic Narcissist will take advantage of the hedonistic atmosphere for his own purposes. You can except a handsome man to sidle up to you during the slow ballads and slide a tendril around you.

Libraries – too boring and not attracting his kind so the Somatic Narcissist is absent as again is the Victim Narcissist. The Cerebral and Elite Narcissists will find willing targets who tick the relevant trait checklist for them and with whispered authority they will demonstrate their intellectual superiority to a waiting pool of targets who are very much aligned with the required traits of the Cerebral and Elite Narcissists.

Sporting Events - too much effort for the Victim Narcissist and nobody likely to be interested in the Cerebral Narcissist leaves the field clear for the Somatic and Elite Narcissists. The roar of the crowd, the demonstration of sporting excellence be it technical (say a grand prix) or physical (athletics) will attract the type of targets that appeal to both the Somatic and Elite Narcissists. Shared interests in physical pursuits and sport will allow choice targets to present themselves and enable both of these narcissists ample opportunity to assess their targets. If the sporting event is one where the narcissist is able to participate then we will gladly avail ourselves of the opportunity to compete and excel. This lends itself to the Somatic Narcissist who finds the arena of sport an excellent showcase for his talents and a fertile place for gathering targets.

Debating Society – any form of debating society or discussion group, for example a book club will provide the Cerebral Narcissist with an open platform from which he may exert his intellectual superiority. He will also find plenty of potential targets amongst those attending as he gathers fuel from the assembled members of the group. The Elite Narcissist will also use such gatherings to his advantage and amongst the membership there is significant potential to identify a primary source target and ensnare them. The Cerebral Narcissist will infiltrate such groups in particular since the combination of being provided with a readymade platform from which fuel can be gathered and an assembled group of like-minded individuals will prove irresistible to him or her.

Museums and Art Galleries – Once again this an environment which will appeal to both Cerebral and Elite Narcissists. Whether it is standing before an exhibit and opining as to its merits to those nearby or taking a more involved role as a curator or volunteer who is on hand to dispense plenty of information about the exhibits, there are considerable opportunities for gathering fuel and also identifying targets to secure primary sources and supplementary sources. The Victim and Somatic Narcissists, just like debating societies and book clubs will be nowhere to be seen since the targets that gather in these environments will not have the desired traits.

Arts and Craft Clubs – you may think that the Cerebral Artists would make an appearance here but he regards such places as beneath him and more importantly the people who attend these clubs will not fit the trait matrix for him. Instead it is the Victim Narcissist who will scour these clubs looking for both a primary source and supplementary sources. He has no interest in the actual purpose of the club. He is there to find his source. He will demonstrate his usual incompetence at painting or pottery in order to draw sympathy and assistance from someone who he will then target. The attendees of such clubs are likely to include those who excel at domestic tasks, have a mothering attitude and therefore will prove a viable target for the Victim Narcissist.

Outdoor Pursuits – whether it is climbing mountains, fell running, hiking, camping or white water rafting the Somatic and Elite Narcissist will be engaged in these activities. They will join an appropriate club or organisation which will allow them the platform to demonstrate their physical superiority whilst drawing similar-minded individuals who are bound to be impressed by the Somatic and Elite Narcissists' stamina and go-getting attitude and thus will provide plenty of scope for the acquisition of a primary source and supplementary sources. It is worth mentioning that the Somatic Narcissist will consider being involved in organisations such as mountain rescue or the Royal National Lifeboat Institution as the opportunities to again showcase his talents and receive fuel from grateful people who he has come to the aid of will prove opportune for him. He does not care about helping people, he solely recognises that their relief and gratitude at being rescued from peril will provide a bond and therefore a viable target for his quest to secure that primary source. Similarly, Somatic Narcissists can be found in the emergency services where the preponderance of situations to act the hero and drink in all that admiring and relieved fuel will prove very tempting.

Shopping Mall - beneath the Elite Narcissist, too much like hard work and of no use to the Cerebral Narcissist it is only the Somatic Narcissist who will regard the retail the experience as one where there is capacity for gaining fuel and acquiring supplemental sources. He may even acquire a primary source by way of a shop assistant from one of the glamorous and expensive stores he frequents who admires his taste in clothes, his looks and his spending power.

The Neighbourhood - The Somatic, Victim and Elite Narcissists regard their locality and especially their neighbours as targets for supplementary sources and gaining a primary source. The Cerebral Narcissist finds neighbourly chit chat and gossip over the garden fence beneath him and there are better places for him to find his targets. The Victim Narcissist will see those who live nearby as people who are obliged to help him and he will repeatedly be seeking the assistance of others with his maintenance chores and such like. He will make great play of bemoaning his lack of culinary skills and domestic ability in order to rope in a neighbour or three to sympathise and provide him with meals from time to time or to invite him to dinner. He will exhibit no shame in telling them how it is a microwave meal for one again in the hope of being invited into their home where he will outstay his welcome as he endeavours to ensnare the target. The Somatic Narcissist will ensure the displays of mowing the lawn whilst shirtless, carrying out maintenance chores with obvious effectiveness, washing the sports car and riding around the neighbourhood regularly will invite admiration and the acquisition of supplementary sources. He will also see if the neighbours have a primary source amongst them, single or desperate housewife. It is the Elite Narcissist who loves the neighbourhood the most as not only is he able to engage in tasks similar to the Somatic Narcissist but he becomes a pillar of the local community through orchestrating events and campaigns (but getting others to do the hard work) for the benefit of the community. He has no interest in doing this other than the admiration he will receive from the acquired supplementary sources and the opportunity to draw in a fellow committee member as a primary source.

Charity Organisations - The Elite and Victim Narcissist prefer this environment whether it is a soup kitchen, a charity shop or organising committee of a charity, these two narcissists will be seeking targets but doing so from opposite positions. The Elite Narcissist will use this environment to draw fuel from the admiration of others for his charitable works. Useful in maintaining the façade, the Elite Narcissist will occupy himself in the organisational element of the charities, dictating to others what should be done and then grabbing the glory. Photo opportunities, pieces in the press and on television will all appeal to him and in doing so he can acquire his supplemental sources whilst securing a primary source from a company the charity has partnered with or from a fellow committee member. He is the grand master who has descended to get the charity ship shape and effective. He has no interest in helping people, the platform is there for his greater glorification and the presentation of targets.

The Victim Narcissist will be looking to find the caring and nurturing people that such organisations attract. He may present himself as a charity case seeking handouts and the assistance and sympathy of those who work for the charity in order to acquire supplemental sources and find a primary source amongst them. He may volunteer to help out in a charity shop or at an animal rescue shelter. He will do very little actual work instead spending his time recalling his own problems and relying on the numerous caring people who volunteer to take pity on him and take him under their wing and become a primary source.

Swimming Pools - whether it is as participant or an overseeing life guard then the aquatic environment provides an ideal opportunity for both Somatic and Elite Narcissists. Drawing admiring glances from other swimmers for that honed physique and the opportunity to sit at the edge of the pool and ensnare that tanned hard body you have seen here every Thursday evening for the last four weeks provides a fertile place for the Elite and especially Somatic Narcissists to find primary sources. The Elite will gravitate more to the lifeguard role, regarding this hero position as befitting his status. The Somatic will see the pool as a place to show off his stamina and especially a place to strut and exhibit his peacock feathers. You may smell chlorine when you go swimming but these narcissists smell only fuel and opportunity to identify targets.

Gym – The playground of the Somatic and Elite Narcissists. Where better to find a host of fuel source targets (both primary and supplementary)? From other users who admire our efforts on the treadmill, our honed physiques and the period of time we plank for through to the regular attendees who we strike up a conversation with over shared interests. Getting someone to spot for us as they encourage us and admire the weight we bench press to the staff and instructors who we can engage with. We may appear to help other gym users out but this is all part of the act of ensnaring these people. Surrounded by others who share an interest in the body beautiful the Somatic Narcissist will prowl the gym (along with fitness classes and such like) where he hopes to find a primary source target from all of the targets on offer.

Swingers' Clubs – Once again the preserve of the Somatic and Elite Narcissists who will easily infiltrate such organisations by reason of their attractiveness, their high sex drives and the ease by which they will charm someone to accompany them to such a club if this a pre-requisite. The Somatic Narcissist will revel in the exhibitionism that he can indulge in here. Multiple partners who will all provide him with fuel for his stamina and technique. Observers who will fuel him by reason of admiration whether real of begrudged. The Somatic and Elite Narcissists will easily be able to sense those attendees who have been brought by their partner rather than necessarily being an enthusiastic attendee and it is those individuals that the Somatic and Elite Narcissists will home in on as they will regard such a target as perfect for their primary source. Compliant, driven by sex but moreover a need to please and no doubt carrying many of the class and special traits which the Somatic and Elite Narcissists covet.

Social Media – All cadres of narcissist use social media as hunting grounds. Social media provides all manner of opportunities for our kind to gather supplementary sources of fuel and then obtain a primary source. Social media allows us access to a massive pool of targets. It provides us with a wealth of information about those targets which we can use to our advantage (which I describe in the next chapter). It enables us to keep a number of targets in play given the reach of social media. It allows us to maintain the provision of fuel and interaction with these targets often through the advances of technology. We can assess a target and quickly move on to another if need be knowing that our reach is great and extensive. A bar may provide perhaps a score of targets for our kind but through social media there are millions of targets. The overarching reason however why our kind use social media as a hunting ground is because it allows us to be absolutely that thing you wish us to be. We can fabricate details about our job, qualifications, looks, achievements and so forth in order to impress and ensnare. False pictures can be used taken from other profiles, false details provided from elsewhere and this fakery allows us to charm. Of course such an approach works best for supplementary sources since meeting in real life would shatter the image. Where we regard someone we find online as a target to be a primary source we use the advantages of the internet to polish up who we are so our most favourable face is provided. We can of course continue to ply certain lies to you, about interests and our past, our earnings (within a degree of stretch) as on meeting us you will are unlikely to be able to dispel those things but most of all by engaging with targets this way we are able to charm and ensnare. We are able to create the image of the person you want so much by exaggerating and highlighting so that you believe in it and want then to meet us. By careful accentuation we are able to create the image you desire and still deliver when we secure meeting you in the flesh. By then and ensuring we have already begun our manipulation of you, you will have succumbed to our charm and therefore once we meet you, you will already be spellbound and want us all the more once you are exposed to our continued seduction. The world of social media is a dangerous place for people like you and it is a happy hunting ground for the likes of us. It is especially favoured by the Cerebral Narcissist as he can use his ability with words, his knowledge and seductive posts to maximum effect through social media. Similarly, the Victim Narcissist can use it to mask certain shortcomings and develop a hold over the target (remembering he will choose someone who will want to care and nurture) so that even when they meet him and he may not be all they imagined (he will not have exaggerated but rather kept quiet certain shortcomings) they will still want him based on the established connection and their need to mother. "Okay, he is plumper than I thought and his car is rather beat-up but he just needs some tweaking from me and he will scrub up just fine," you will think and he knows this. The nature of the internet allows us to be more pliable with the truth that usual and we will have you hooked before you know it. Even when you meet us, even if everything is not quite as special as you thought (and this is not always the case, often you will be even more blown away when you do finally meet us) you will still be sufficiently hooked to move forward with us because we know you are the type of person who will and most of all many of your kind have a real problem saying 'no'. Somatic and Elite narcissist make extensive use of social media but they like to move things quickly to actually meeting up as it is in the flesh that they can exhibit their peacock feathers better than anybody else and therefore increase their prospects of ensnaring you.

It is particularly pertinent to point out that the most dangerous place on social media is where you belong to support groups. Those groups which provide a place for people to learn more about those who have abused them, swap war stories, support one another, pour hate on their abusers and generally have a good old rant and complain are ideal places for our kind. They are easy to infiltrate and they are teeming with exactly the type of people who will tick many of the required trait criteria because they have been caught by our kind previously. We already know they fit the bill by their presence and it is all a case of weeding out members of our brethren who are lurking there (I spot them readily enough should they break cover) and then identifying the relevant person who can then be approached in person. By spending time in these forums we know all the correct things to state as we mimic people like you and it is no difficulty at all for us to pass as one of you as we gather information and you, thinking you have a kindred spirit, share details readily. The lesser functioning of my kind tend to show their true colours by lashing out at other forum members. I am content for them to do so as it acts as a diversion, allows me to attack the interloper (thus increasing my own credentials and legitimacy) and leaves me well placed to exact my manipulative information gathering as I see fit. Sometimes I will just remain in the group in order to learn more to use in the real world and not interact with the members of the group, other times I will interact, mimicking them and creating my own back story for the purposes of evoking sympathy and camaraderie and then it is a case of waiting for the right individual to come swimming too close to where I am waiting.

It is not just those support groups which cater for the victims of our kind. There are groups for being who have been abused generally (whether by one of our kind or not) and therefore there are shoals of individuals who are likely to fulfil the criteria, particularly the damaged special trait criterion. There are groups for those suffering from personality disorders, such as borderline personality disorder or histrionic personality disorder which also provide hunting grounds for finding targets who fit the criteria and again fulfil the criteria of being damaged and/or challenging so beloved of the elite of our kind. These places are like universities for us to learn more, gather information and then line-up the choice cuts for us to select.

You should be extremely vigilant of who you are dealing with when you join one of these support groups. You never truly know who you are interacting with or who is just waiting in the shadows gathering information to use elsewhere.

Social media is a place full of traps for your kind. We exist in sizeable numbers as we swim through cyberspace waiting to identify the many targets that are just sitting there waiting.

Dating Sites – much of that which I have written above concerning social media is equally applicable to dating sites on the internet and accordingly every cadre of narcissist will use dating sites to identify targets. Moreover, every cadre of narcissist prefers dating sites for one particular reason. The targets are sitting ducks. These people are wanting a relationship. This mind set makes them susceptible to being ensnared as they are approaching the interaction with the idea of becoming that person's intimate partner. There is plenty of scope for gathering supplementary fuel sources through dating sites – frequent dates and someone becoming an outer or inner circle friend even if they do not make the grade as a primary source. Most of all this is where primary sources will be found. The targets have the right mind set, they detail what they like (thus we can adjust ourselves and reflect what you want to say), they detail what they do not like (thus we can avoid those things and mask them) and through this disclosure we can also gauge whether they fulfil the relevant class traits that suit us and also the generic and special traits. There is huge scope for fuel and manipulation along with the gathering of a primary source target and thus the internet dating site, combined with the points I made above concerning social media, means that it is like shooting fish in a barrel. You really are a sitting target when you go on a dating site and you are placing yourself in the sights of the narcissist when you do this.

Our kind lurks everywhere. We can turn most environments to our advantage should our sensitive antennae detect the presence of a target. Since we like to be economical with our energy however we look for our supplementary sources and especially our primary sources in key environments as I have described above. Now you know which type of narcissist you attract, you know the places where you are at greater risk of their presence and of being a target.

Having ascertained what, we look for in our targets and where we mainly find these targets how do we then go about choosing our targets? How do we approach them and ascertain sufficient information about this target so we then begin our seduction? This is the topic of our next chapter as we look at how we target our victims.

5. How We Target Our Victims?

This is the masterclass in the gaining of information about the person we have in our sights so we know they are a viable target for our seduction. This is how we ascertain whether the person is someone we should pursue and also how we know they will be a waste of time and therefore should be left alone. There is often preparatory work undertaken before we have even contacted you or spoken to you and then we are engaged in drawing information from you (both spoken and from the way you behave) which confirms to us that you have the generic, class and hopefully the special traits too. Your presence in the environment is of course a key indicator and something which suggests that you are more likely than not going to tick the class traits but we also need you to fulfil the generic traits also. Occasionally there are people in an environment who would not normally be there and we must weed out these anomalies so we can focus on the better targets. We will look at the various steps we take and also demonstrate how these are used in certain environments that I have detailed above so you are able to recognise how we will approach you and target you.

This is not about the way we seduce you. That is for a different time. This is about what we do when we are targeting you prior to the seduction commencing. Inevitably, where we make contact with you to gather more intelligence to ascertain whether you are a viable contact, there will be a degree of charm and the seduction will commence. If we gauge you not to be a good target then this will be broken off although given our background checks and the environmental situation that we have chosen, this is rare. However, keep in mind that this is about the way we target you and how we do so.

5.1 An Existing Connection

This consideration is mainly applicable to a primary source target. We love there to be an existing connection between us. This might be that we work for the same company, visit the same gym, buy our coffee in the same coffee shop or take the same time train each day. Even better is if the existing connection is historic, for example that we went to school or college together or that we were neighbours some time ago. The purpose of an existing connection is threefold: -

1. We are likely to know some information about you already. If it is historic there is a greater chance of this and even by virtue of the fact, we are repeatedly in the same environment (although you may not have noticed us) we are able to gather intelligence about you;
2. We have an easy opportunity to make contact with you; and
3. Most importantly it allows us to use our harpoon.

We will know about some of your interests and this will allow us to check them against our trait requirements. This also provides us with material to use when we approach you. We have seen how you behave, most likely have spoken to you and this existing connection provides us with an early opportunity to gather information about you.

Consider when the narcissist you became entangled with first approached you. Chances are that within the first meeting or shortly thereafter, he or she will have said something similar to,
"I have loved you for ten years ever since we were at college."
"You won't realise but I have adored you every day for the last six years."
"I have been in love with you ever since you lived along the street from me."

This is the harpoon. It is our way of crashing through your defences and driving a harpoon into your heart so you are ensnared and all we need to do is haul you towards us. The harpoon must be of sufficient intensity to achieve its aim and a declaration of so far unrequited love that has burned away from afar for years is one method of achieving this. It takes you by surprise, flatters you and makes you feel strangely obligated towards us. Goodness me, he has loved me for six years and I never knew, that is amazing, I feel flattered but also as if I have to reciprocate in some way. That is often the reaction of those who have been subjected to this harpoon. Accordingly, we like to have an existing connection as this not only helps in ascertaining your viability as a target (we know something about you already) but it starts the seduction rolling as well.

5.2 The Background Checks

If there is an existing connection, we will still undertake this work prior to making an approach. If there is no existing connection, then this preparatory work becomes all the more important. We carry this out for two main reasons: -

1. First and foremost, to gauge whether you will make a viable target; and
2. To provide us with material to use when we approach you.

What do these background checks encompass?

a. Friends

We will use your friends to find out more about you. These people may already be our friends or at least acquaintances and therefore pumping them for information will prove easy. If your friends are not already known to us, we will ascertain who they are. We will make a note of who you are socialising with say in a bar and look for an opportune moment to approach them. We may wait until you have left or alternatively approach one of your friends under the auspices of being interested in him or her and through careful questioning find out more about you. We will be looking to learn how long they have known you for, how they know you, other places you go to together, where you live, whether you are in a relationship and what your interests are. For instance, during the conversation with one of your friends we may ask the following: -

"Which other bars do you go to?"

(We find out where else we might find you and when)

"Have you been to x restaurant?"

(Gauging whether this is popular or not amongst your group. We will ask about other types of restaurant and ask whether you all go there together.)

"Do you live near one another? Yes, where about is that then? Oh yes I know it, do you live near x, no? The other side. What's that street called? Yes, that's right."

"How long have you been friends? Since school? Which school was that? All of you except (you as the target are pointed out) I see where did Alison(target) go?"

"So are you all attached ladies?" (This will allow the friends to confirm their statuses – "We three are but Alison and Julie are free agents." This will allow us to gauge more about that situation, "Nobody good enough for them eh?"

Someone will most likely tell us why they are single, their choice in men, that they had a messy break-up or they have decided not to date for a while.

I will provide an example of how this is done in such an environment below. If we are friends with your friends already our questioning will be more detailed as the need for subtlety will be reduced. This will enable us to obtain more specific information for our use. We may approach your family as well to provide us with additional information although this can prove more difficult than approaching your friends. If we happen to know your family reasonably well, for instance they still live in the same house that you lived in when we knew you from college and our parents live nearby, we may "pop" round just to say hello and find out where you are living these days, working and other information about your personal life which could be asked in a normal and polite conversation.

b Lieutenants

Our trusty and loyal lieutenants will be used to gather intelligence for our use. They are used in the following ways: -

- Approaching you and gathering information under the auspices of chatting you up;
- Approaching you and gathering information under the auspices of a survey. This method in particular is useful for ascertaining your traits without you realising what is really happening;
- Following you to find out where you work and/or live;
- Speaking to your friends and other people who know you in order to gather information you;
- Undertaking searches of records and such like in order to find out information about you. For instance, we may have a lieutenant who works for the bank at which you bank and he can provide us with details about your address and also your spending habits, for example you spend repeatedly in a florists or at a beauty salon. The lieutenant may work at your utility company, a local authority which has details about you and so on whereby they will provide the necessary information to us.

- Following you on the same day for say three weeks so we get a picture of your daily habits – where you get a newspaper from, which gym you attend, how you get to work, who else you speak to on the journey, where you meet a friend for lunch, where you work, where you go shopping, which class you attend the evening, the type of car you might drive. This not only provides us with plenty of information about the type of things that you do so we can gauge them against our traits checklist but it then also provides an opportunity for the lieutenant to approach the third party and find out more about you. For instance, if our lieutenant has not been able to follow you to work he may enter the café where you have just been and pretend you left your purse behind and ask the counter assistant where he might find you to hand it back to her. Most people are obliging and will want to help and will explain where you work to our lieutenant who can then make further enquiries there on our behalf but also ensure he picks up the trail there again.
- Dating you or rather pretending to go on a date with you but really it is an information gathering exercise with prepared questions to determine your suitability against the Generic, Class and Special Traits. You should be wary of those you date as the Dating Lieutenant is a key method of targeting you. There is no immediate threat because the Lieutenant is engaged in completing his or her role for me, they have no real interest in you. They have done this many times and will have a degree of charm about them. The Dating Lieutenant will be pleasant and you will enjoy the date but there will only ever be two dates. One to gather information and the second to clarify anything which arose from the first if you remain a viable target. We do not alert you to our presence by approaching you directly and we get to save our energies by the use of one of our Lieutenants to do this work for us. You should remain wary of those who you date. You may think he is asking a lot of questions

because he is interested in you. You are right. He is interested but not for the reason you think. His puppet master is waiting in the background to pour over the acquired knowledge you have freely given up. I find the Dating Lieutenant a real Trojan horse when it comes to targeting my next prospect and the establishment of loyal and effective Lieutenants takes on all the more importance because of this role that they play on my behalf.

The use of Lieutenants (and we will most likely use more than one in our information gathering when we target you) allows us to achieve the following: -

- Gathering plenty of information about you to use against our trait checklist;
- Gathering plenty of information about you to assist our approach to you;
- Allowing us to gather more information in a shorter space of time by having additional people help us
- Avoid the risk of alerting you by us approaching you and others at an early stage
- Enabling us to conserve our resources;
- Preventing us from getting our hands dirty

Accordingly, lieutenants are widely used and crucial in carrying out these background checks.

c Social Media

Not only is social media a happy hunting ground for us, it also provides us with an opportunity to gather more information about you. In all seriousness if you knew how much our kind uses social media to further our advances you would go nowhere near it. It allows us to select targets, it allows us to gather information as to their suitability and provides an effective tool by which we seduce you. Thereafter social media is instrumental in devaluing you before Hoovering you and the provision of information about what you are doing and where you have gone when we are seeking to locate you for the purposes of that Hoover. It is one of the deadliest inventions and allows our kind to manipulate and gather our fuel with impunity.

We may take a picture and conduct an image search to find a similar picture of you. The easiest way to do this is to have one of our lieutenants (or we may do it) take a picture of you and your friends together using their cameras and phones and then some of you alone and some of you with your friends on our phone. There is a high chance that you or your friends will upload the pictures of your night out or your day trip to a social media site and our very similar picture taken seconds later will link to the first and then we will find you or your friends first, which will then lead to you.

Once we have located you on social media we will comb through your accounts on Facebook Twitter, LinkedIn, Instagram and so forth gathering two types of information: -

1. Information to use against our trait checklists; and

2. Information which may assist us in finding out more about you (e.g. where you work so a Lieutenant can be dispatched to that workplace) and to assist us when we approach you.

We will note places, photographs, likes, people you are friends with, the people you follow and who follow you, the nature of comments, interests, places you have visited and so on in order to compile this body of information for the above two purposes.

We will use an established false profile (which will have been in place for some time, have various friends/followers and plenty of ephemeral postings, Tweets etc., or a false resume (LinkedIn) to create an air of authenticity. We will send a friend request, follow you and so forth in order to gain further access to your social media profile. We will not at this stage engage with you because we are still in the process of assimilating information to help with that stage. This preparatory work is all about checking that you fit our needs as a target and providing us with information and material by which we can make an approach.

D Observation

We will also spend some time watching you. You will not notice that we are doing this. This is done perhaps when we know you go to the same bar after work every Thursday or dine at a particular restaurant or café. It may be a case of joining a class which you attend and watching you there or at the gym. It will usually be the case that this observation is done when other people are around so that we are inconspicuous. Standing outside your house and place of work may prove to be too obvious and we will leave that to our Lieutenants to do instead. By observing you we can see what you eat and drink, the routines you engage in, the other people you engage with and how you engage with them. Are you sociable? Are you someone who is content with your own company and a book as you sit in the sunshine outside the office at lunchtime? Do you get drunk easily? Are you talkative or someone who listens more than speaks? We are well-practised as ascertaining characters and studying behaviour and therefore spending some time observing you provides us with additional information to ascertain whether you are a viable target or not.

Accordingly, these are the main background checks that we will undertake to confirm whether we think you are a suitable target and prior to us making an approach where we deem that to be in our best interests. What then are we looking for when we are undertaking these background checks? Naturally we want to ascertain whether you will make an excellent primary source of fuel and to do this we need to see which of the relevant traits you exhibit from the generic and class categories. We will also look for traits in the special category although it tends to be the case that these are better ascertained from our direct contact. This initial background stage enables us to decide whether you have few traits and therefore are probably a poor prospect and we should save our energy and move on to somebody else or whether you exhibit a number of traits which merits further assessment through approaching you. What will we be looking for then in terms of specific indicators for the relevant traits?

6. The Generic Traits

Love Devotee - at this stage we will look for information you have relayed to a lieutenant about previous relationships and whether you were left heartbroken. We will look for inspirational quotes which you retweet and plaster on your Facebook timeline which show you are a great believer in love. We will look for certain films, books and music in your interests which show that you are a love devotee. *Wuthering Heights, Ghost, Four Weddings and a Funeral, PS I Love You, The Notebook* and *Pretty Woman* are ones which I find to be good indicators of love devotion. A useful indicator is the posting of songs late at night as this tells me that you are sat alone, possibly drunk, mourning the loss of a past love or wishing that you were with somebody. The nature of the songs is instructive as well. Wistful, dreamy love songs indicate considerable love devotion. 'Angry' songs which espouse recovery and independent for example the archetypal *I Will Survive* or *Single Ladies* is more indicative of being potentially damaged and hurting or a challenging individual and satisfies alternative criteria. We will observe which groups you belong to on Facebook as these prove highly instructive in terms of telling us which traits you may have. Recovery and survivors' groups indicate damage. Groups that exchange quotes about love indicates love devotion. We ascertain the things you have liked as these provide additional indicators. Your comments on other postings also prove of assistance. If a friend has posted about being upset about a failed relationship and you comment along the lines of "Love conquers all", "there is somebody out there for everybody" or the old favourite "plenty more fish in the sea" then you are a clear love devotee. The blurb on dating profiles also provides us with an excellent insight into whether you are a love devotee or not. Making reference to romantic nights in together, having been hurt but still want to find that special person, the desire to look for your prince charming or knight in shining armour are all prime indicators of you being a love devotee.

Compassion- do you regularly share posts of a child in hospital and type "Amen" underneath? Do we see that you set up justgiving appeals? If you post pictures of you taking part in a run for a cancer charity or doing a sponsored skydive for the local hospice we know that the compassion trait is being ticked. From exhibit sympathetic posts and tweets when you learn of a friend suffering some misfortune through to the even greater indicator of you expressing your feelings about a tragedy where you do not even know the victims, these tell us that you are a compassionate person. We may see you in a café comforting an upset friend or observe you giving money or a sandwich to the homeless person outside your office. Our Lieutenants may learn of your volunteer work at a nearby school or find out that you have moved in with an infirm parent to nurse them.

If you are an animal lover this is a big tick for this trait. Posting lots of photographs of your dog or cat, expressing horror at the latest picture of a big game hunter with his or her kill, posting and sharing animal and charity welfare information all tell us that you are an animal lover and therefore compassionate. We may see you walking your dog or notice a cat prowling lounging on your porch or car bonnet. We may see you buying animal feed in the supermarket, notice your car smells of dog or has scratch marks on the rear showing where they clamber in and out when you take them for a walk. We may observe dog hairs on your jumper when we are near to you. Bumper stickers are often a good way to determine whether you are animal lover. Anything which shows you have a love for animals confirms to us that you are a compassionate person.

Naturally if we know you work in nursing, a care home for the elderly, volunteer at an animal rescue shelter and so on we know you positively ooze with compassion.

Decency – we observe the way that you conduct yourself in public. Do you open doors for people, have good manners, act in a polite fashion? Do you ensure your children behave themselves when in a restaurant for example? We will observe whether you provide a tip to the waiting staff, whether you make complaints over nothing or praise good service. Will you help an elderly person with their bags or offer them a seat on public transport? Are your Facebook posts free of bragging and slagging matches with other people ensuring you never air your dirty linen in public and that you have no need to boast about your achievements? We pay particular regard to what your friends say about you and especially when you are not there. Do they sing your praises or will they snipe about you hogging the conversation, not paying your share of the bill or failing to return something you had borrowed? We are able to pick up lots of snippets of information about the way you behave and conduct yourself from your friends, by use of our Lieutenants, from social media and simple observation to ascertain whether we would regard you as a decent person.

Moral Compass - we want to see if you have a strong moral compass and that you understand right from wrong. Would you tell someone they have given you too much change in a shop? Would you hand in a wallet that you have found outside without taking anything from it? Do we see you express concern and indignation through your social media about travesties that take place around the world or are such comments absent? Do we see you setting a good example for your children in the way that you behave? Are their rumours about you stealing, falsifying expenses or engaging in loose behaviour? Are you known for your fidelity in your relationships? Are you regarded as a loyal and dependable friend? Would your friends consider you somebody who does the right thing in a certain situation? Our Lieutenants will take an opportunity to telephone you or stop you in the street and ask you a set of hypothetical questions concerning moral issues as part of a supposed survey. The fact you stop and give your time to participate provides a tick under decency above and then we are able to analyse your answers to gauge whether you have a strong moral compass or not.

Caring – we will look to see whether you have children, whether you look after elderly and/or ill relatives and also whether you have pets (see above). Do you donate to charities? When we sit near you do we hear you always asking other people how they are before sharing your news? Have we observed you assisting someone who needs help or is in distress? Would you pick up a piece of litter? Do we see that you recycle and travel to work by bicycle because you care about the environment? Do we have any knowledge about your involvement in community issues because you care about the neighbourhood? Is your job one of the caring vocations? Are your tweets all about you and never about anybody else? Are your Facebook posts a compilation of duck-faced selfies where nobody else gets a look in? These are additional indicators that assist us in determine whether you are a caring person or not.

Honest – some of the indicators I described with reference to decency are applicable here. My Lieutenants will ascertain whether you tell lies. I will engineer a situation for a lieutenant to drop something of value to see if you tell him and hand it to him or whether you keep it for yourself. Our Lieutenants will feed you some information which is detrimental to one of your friends and will ascertain whether you will tell your friend about this information or not.

Need to Understand – do we notice that you spend time with people as they explain something so you understand what has happened? Do we see from the books that you like and read that they exhibit a need to comprehend things? Do you post a picture of some atrocity and comment that you cannot understand why somebody would act like that? We will arrange for a Lieutenant to be unpleasant to you and then ascertain whether you will contact him or her to try and sort things out and ascertain what happened. Do we know whether you read self-help books or subscribe to certain YouTube channels which are based on recovery or self-improvement? These are the type of indicators we will be looking for as part of our background checks.

Underdog – have we or our Lieutenants witnessed you intervene on the side of somebody who is being unfairly treated? Are you involved in campaigns to better the position of minority groups? Do you use social media to highlight social injustice and trumpet the cause of the underdog? Do your supporting inclinations indicate that you support a less successful (even unsuccessful) sports team when a bigger and more successful rival would be the easier choice? Do you exhibit a tendency in your dealings with people, the situations you are in and the choices you make to support the less advantaged person or group? Are you an advocate (whether professional or lay) for those who are not able to speak for themselves? Not only does these indicators support the notion of you being caring, compassionate and decent they also show to us that you are on the side of the underdog.

Strive for the Truth – do you engage with people in a truthful manner without necessarily being blunt and hurtful? Are you able to find a way to convey an uncomfortable truth in a way that assists the recipient? Do you listen carefully and probe what someone is saying in order to get to the bottom of the matter and establish what the truth is? Have we heard you comment or seen you post about media articles which you disagree with? Have you raised questions about miscarriages of justice? Do you regularly promote accountability and transparency either through the things you say or post about or through your membership of particular organisations and the actions you take? All of these are indicators of that empathic quality of striving for the truth which we prefer to have in those we target.

Excellent Listener - are you the one who listens attentively to what someone else is saying? Our Lieutenants will test you by talking about a subject and then asking you questions about what has been said in order to determine whether you have been paying attention. In a group situation can we see you hogging the limelight and talking over people or are you content to sit and listen, chipping in occasionally? Can we see you are thoughtful when being spoken to? When we review your exchanges on social media can we see that you are taking on board the other person's point of view or are you behaving in a bullish fashion and missing the thrust of what the other person is saying? Will you admit to changing your opinion in the face of what somebody else is saying? Have we seen you at lectures paying rapt attention to what the speaker has been saying or are you fiddling with your 'phone instead?

Accordingly, through the application of our background checks, by engaging with your friends, using our Lieutenants, combing your social media and observing you, we will be seeing whether you comply with the various generic traits that we hold in high regard. Sometimes we are not able to ascertain them all and therefore we will need to rely on our contact with you to achieve this, but we are able to see which way the wind is blowing and determine whether we should move on to contact or look to a different target. Of course, whilst these background checks are being applied to the generic traits they are also being applied to checking which of the class traits you are complying with and so it is to those that we turn.

7. The Class Traits

7.1 The Victim Narcissist

Physical appearance – the Victim Narcissist will easily observe your physical appearance to ensure that the target is not physically imposing compared to him, not or considerable attractiveness so that he or she might prove tempting to somebody else.

Consummate Care Giver - the Victim Narcissist will be looking for evidence of involvement in the healthcare sector, references on social media or through friends to caring for a sick relative or an elderly family member. This narcissist will also seek out evidence of the target being an animal lover. He will check on social media what the occupation of the target is to ascertain whether he or she is in the caring professions. He will be particularly interested in those who operate in the sectors where it is necessary to care for the elderly, the disabled and the terminally ill.

Lack of interest in looks – the Victim Narcissist will ascertain from combing social media is the target has a fixation with looks and physical appearance. If there are numerous selfies, pictures of shoes and clothing, he will not regard the person as a viable target unless many of the other criteria are met. A compassionate nurse who likes shoes and handbags will be acceptable to him. He will look for those who share posts about "Beauty being on the inside" and "Love is more than looks". He will sit and observe his target to see if they take more than a passing interest in somebody who is good-looking who comes their way. If this narcissist has access to a handsome lieutenant, he will ensure this Lieutenant engages with the target to gauge their reaction to his looks.

Mothering Nature - the Victim Narcissist will be looking for two things here through his background checks. Firstly, he will ascertain whether the target is a mother. Accordingly, he will observe whether she has children with her and if so how she deals with them. Is she fussing over them, keeping them entertained, wiping their noses and so on? If so this ticks, this particular indicator. Secondly, he will be looking for evidence of domestication. Someone who regularly posts pictures of the cakes they have baked on social media will appeal to him. Someone who shows the results of their needlecraft, sewing or knitting or exhibits membership of groups which engage in such activity will result in this criteria being fulfilled. Comments on Facebook such as "Just cleaned the house from top to bottom, shattered but no rest for me, garden next!" will attract his interest. If the targets home is known, he will organise for a lieutenant to peer in through the windows of if possible even get inside (lawfully) to see how well-kept it is. Observations such as a laundry often being on the line (including bedding – which shows the bedding is changed regularly) will confirm to this narcissist that the target is domesticated and cares about the nest before anything else.

Not a high achiever – any boasts about repeated successes at work, in sports, in intellectual pursuit, in clubs and such like will lessen the attraction for this narcissist. He will monitor social media posts for this type of information, ascertain from friends whether the target belongs to such clubs and organise day-to-day activity.

Lack of interest in money/status – the Victim Narcissist will want to ensure that conversations and social media are not centred on money and possessions. Instead he will be looking for comments which are more about family, birthdays, anniversaries and such like showing the homeward and family orientated nature of the target.

Giver not a receiver - the Victim Narcissist will most likely utilise a Lieutenant to question the target on such matters but this is something that is more likely ascertained form contact.

Low sex drive – again the Victim Narcissist will elicit this information during contact but there are some early indicators. An absence of discussions about men and sex in person and on social media, the absence of pictures of the naked torsos of men or bikini clad beach babes will start to reassure this narcissist that the target does not have an excessive interest in sex nor a high sex drive.

Companionship - through observation the Victim Narcissist will want to see that the target values having family visit for meals and would rather do this than go out somewhere. Social media should contain plenty of comments about family members, family members will form many (if not the majority) of the target's social media friends and followers. Photographs will be of family occasions, Christmas, birthdays and such like and all again within the home. Posting comments about missing a deceased family member will also be viewed favourably, along with remembering that person through pictures, postings on their birthday and the anniversary of their death.

Few Outside Interests – the Victim Narcissist will want to ensure through questioning by Lieutenants, observation of the daily routine of the target and a thorough comb of his or her social media that the target is not involved with going out a lot, having membership of lots of different clubs and organisations which will pull him or her away from the home where he or she should be caring for and providing attention to the Victim Narcissist.

Lack of stimulus – the target should not have much regard for the influence of the outside world. They are unlikely to read newspapers, do not post political comment and if questioned about their views about say a particular political campaign or tax increases they will shrug and claim not to know much about it. Their focus needs to be on the home and in turn the Victim Narcissist so there needs to be an absence of interests which might attract somebody other than this narcissist.

Children – the Victim Narcissist will look for evidence of children either through observation or discussion with friends. He will check social media for references to children and also photographs and such like. If there are no children, he will organise for a Lieutenant to question the target about the desire to have children, perhaps striking up a conversation in a park where children are playing nearby and commenting about how great they are and ascertaining the target's response. The Victim Narcissist has no interested in the existing children, he just wants to know about their existence because this indicates a mothering character and a home bird. If there are no existing children he will be interested to know if the target would want children as one of his early aims will be to get his target pregnant once the seduction is on foot.

7.2 The Cerebral Traits

Appreciation of knowledge – have we seen you reading books and newspapers? Do you attend lectures, tour museums and art galleries? Does your social media profile demonstrate that you like to visit places of interest and share this? Do we see that you ask questions about events? Our Lieutenants will be used to question you to find out if you have a thirst for knowledge, whether there are any books in your house or whether you are glued to the television set.

Interest in the wider world - we will listen in on your conversations to ascertain whether they are about current affairs, politics, religion and the like or whether it is mundane celebrity gossip and a fascination with having your nails coloured. Once again we will look on your social media profile to ascertain whether you are a supporter of pressure groups. We will organise a lieutenant to share a quiz to you which will detail your knowledge of countries or say capital cities or famous landmarks to gauge whether you look at the world around you or walk around with your eyes closed.

Intellectual capability - in addition to listening in on the nature of your conversations to gauge this, we will see what your education history is on your Facebook profile, we will even organise to find out your qualifications and exam results to ascertain that firstly you have the intellectual capability to provide fuel and a stimulus to us but secondly that you will not outshine us. It is one thing to find you tick the criteria but quite another if that tick is larger than ours. Lieutenants will conduct a supposed survey with you which consists of questions which will elicit your level of intellect. We will scour your social media in the hope of finding classic literature amongst your reading rather than colouring books and independent and arthouse cinema as opposed to another Transformers movie in your liked films. Musical tastes will also be ascertained from friends and we will arrange for a Lieutenant to start playing loud music from his phone near to you to gauge a reaction. If you frown at some dance music or start bobbing your head to it, we will have an indication as to your preferences. Of course, any one of those things is not determinative in itself but a whole array of intellectual capability scrutiny is undertaken through observation, questioning your friends, our Lieutenants and going through your social media.

Reading/ Current Affairs – we will observe the books and periodicals that you read, have our Lieutenants report back on this and organise for them to obtain a copy of your lending history if you are a member of a library. The absence of any reference to books will be a large negative factor and is likely to lead to the cerebral narcissist looking elsewhere.

Excellent listener – although this is part of the generic traits, the Cerebral Narcissist will wish to make sure that he will have a rapt and attentive audience from his primary source when he sets the world to rights or opines on a particular topic. To check this, he will send a Lieutenant to issue a lengthy monologue and gauge reaction. We will ascertain whether you attend plays, lectures, opera and such like and that you are able to sit through it without looking dis-interested, fiddling with your phone or talking. You will be observed in a group situation to see if you prefer to do all the talking or whether you are content to listen to somebody else orate. It is important that the target responds and there someone who would just sit and allow their eyes to glaze over as they drifted off imagining their life as a Kardashian would not appeal. Accordingly, through observation and friends we will gauge whether you listen and then respond. If you are a student we will infiltrate your lectures to see if you pay attention to what the lecturer is saying and whether you ask any pertinent and meaningful questions. If you teach, do you listen to what your students have to say. Are you open to the opinion of others or must you always be heard and that you have no time for anybody else's words? Such indicators are important to the Cerebral Narcissist.

Likes Knowledge – The Cerebral Narcissist will be looking for evidence in your conversations, from what is relayed through your friends and dotted over your social media that you attend places which are repositories of knowledge. Visits to important and well-known libraries such as the Library of Congress, the Reading Room of the British Museum, the Bodleian Library in Oxford (UK) or the Vatican Library will be met with approval. We approve of seeing you attend a pub quiz for example and that you perform well in the contest. We like to see you doing crosswords or watching documentaries on television. The Cerebral Narcissist uses this liking of knowledge as firstly an indicator that you will be most interested in him and secondly to ensure you will not outshine him through your extensive knowledge.

Musical – the Cerebral Narcissist enjoys music and is invariably proficient at playing an instrument and therefore will seek to ascertain that his target likes music but also of a similar nature to him. He will look to see if you carry an instrument, look over your shoulder to read your playlist on your iPod and phone, check your social media for postings of songs from YouTube, reference to concerts and musicians that you like. He will ascertain from your friends which artists you like and gauge your musical proficiency. The Cerebral Narcissist wants to ensure you enjoy music and moreover that your preferences are similar to his own. He will of course, during seduction, express great affinity for your type of music but what he really wants to ensure is that you will like what he likes so that when he plays it to you (either by using an instrument or through a device) you will praise him and not criticise his music choice. No narcissist will willingly entice someone who has a basis for criticising him and different music tastes is a key area where this can happen. We do not regard having differing music tastes as just something that happens with two people, the fact that you do not like what we like means that you are inherently criticising us and this will result in an ignition of our fury at an early juncture. Accordingly, ensuring that there is musical compatibility is important.

Plays, films and art - similar considerations are applicable to this trait as detailed in music above. Not only will we apply similar methods to ascertain that you enjoy these intellectual pursuits we are ensuring you will like similar things to us so that when we provide you with our appraisal of the play we have seen at the theatre you will not merely shrug and say "It was alright" but that you will be able to respond in a meaningful and constructive fashion but most of all you will be most appreciative of our critique. We will use our lieutenants to ask you out on a date and suggest suitable places to go to ascertain that you like them and this ticks the criteria. If you turn your nose up at an invitation to watch King Lear and express a preference for watching reality television the Cerebral Narcissist will not regard you as a viable target.

Lack of Physicality - the Cerebral Narcissist will not want someone who is vastly physical superior to him and this is naturally ascertained by observation. Not only is it highly likely that such an individual will like those pursuits and interests which would not gain fuel for the Cerebral Narcissist, they are also less likely (although not necessarily so) going to be less interested in those things that the Cerebral Narcissist excels in and thus the potential for fuel will be vastly reduced. Moreover, when the Cerebral Narcissist begins his cutting and acidic devaluation he does not want someone who could knock him to the ground.

Sociable - the Cerebral Narcissist wants an individual who will listen attentively to his monologues but he also wants someone who is sociable and enables his brilliance by prompting discussion on something which the Cerebral Narcissist will take over and dominate in conversation. He wants someone who can attend dinner parties and provide him with an appreciative audience who will lead the plaudits so that others follow once the Cerebral Narcissist has delivered his ground-shaking observations. Accordingly, the Cerebral Narcissist will observe how you interact with other people, whether you engage in meaningful conversation with them that is above the banal and mundane. He will scrutinise your online conversation and ensure that spelling and grammar are correct, as well as approving the nature of the conversations. He wants someone who can engage in conversation and is of sufficient intellectual ability to engage with him but never eclipse him. He will use Lieutenants to date you over dinner and probe the extent of your knowledge about certain subjects. Indeed, the deployment of a Lieutenant in such a manner will provide a fantastic opportunity to gather details from the target to ascertain her suitability. I have placed listening devices on two of my Lieutenants when I have organised for them to take a target on a dinner date so I could listen in and note down everything they said to ensure nothing was lost in recall and that I was content with the target's level of suitability.

Compliant – the Cerebral Narcissist wishes to ensure that you will agree with his observations, praise them and not be too challenging. This again is something that is ascertained by careful scrutiny of your online conversations, observed real-life conversations and elicited by careful application of a dating Lieutenant.

The Cerebral Narcissist wishes to find a target that enjoys and is interested in knowledge, is sociable and has a good grasp of many of the higher things in life alongside a general interest in the world and what it has to offer. So long as she agrees and praises without outshining, the Cerebral Narcissist will find most if not all of this class' criteria have been met by the target.

7.3 <u>The Somatic Narcissist</u>

Athletic - the Somatic Narcissist will evidently determine athleticism by regarding the target in the flesh. He will also utilise his Lieutenants and the consideration of social media to find evidence of the target belonging to running clubs, athletic clubs, posting how many miles they have run that day with Strava, information about how far they have cycled (and also where – always helpful to then follow you when you post the route along which you cycle and the times).

High Sex Drive - the Somatic Narcissist will consider the way you dress and behave in public as indicators of having a high sex drive. The Dating Lieutenant will be dispatched to gather more information in this regard as specific questioning about your sexual appetite, done in a flirtatious manner will yield the required information. Should we witness you engaging in flirtatious behaviour with other people when we are observing you we will regard this as an indicator (although not an absolute determinant – after all there are plenty of teasers) of a high sex drive. We will peruse your pictures on social media for evidence of posing in front of mirrors, arm across your breasts providing a tempting picture of some cleavage, or pictures of you in a bikini on holiday. An excessive amount of pictures that show you in skimpy outfits, draped around members of the opposite sex and such like are all indicators that we will look out for. We will study your body language when you are with people. Do you look people in the eye a lot, show the inside of your wrists to the, sit close to the person you are with and do you touch them a lot? Again, these are all indicators. We will review your social media for any evidence of quizzes you may have participated in that reinforce your sexual appetite. The Lieutenants will conduct surveys with you on the pretext for it being about some new underwear or sex toy in order to gather information about your sex drive. There are plenty of ways that the Somatic Narcissist will glean how fired-up your libido is.

Omission of books and art - the Somatic Narcissist will not want to see too much evidence of books, plays, theatre, art and such like in your life. If he does, this will lessen his interest in your target unless you score strongly on the other criteria which he values. Occasional references to literature and the arts will be permissible but beyond that it becomes a problem for him as your interest in these traits will no provide anything for him and also deny him various grounds on which to begin his seduction.

Sociable - in a similar way to the fact that the Cerebral Narcissist wants a target that is sociable, so will the Somatic Narcissist. Owing to his need to strut his peacock feather he wants someone to accompany him to all the venues where he can be seen and also someone who will be his admirer-in-chief and be the catalyst for more fuel to flow from those watching. Accordingly, the Somatic Narcissist will be pleased to see a long list of places that you have checked in to on Face Book which are bars, restaurants, concerts and similar. He will want to see plenty of photographs posted showing you out and about at the venues which he likes. He wants to read your tweets about having tickets to the latest pop concert. He will sit and watch you with people to see you flit from one to another, ever the social butterfly and will be delighted to see a timeline chock full of personable if inane discussions with other people as this will all mark you out as a sociable individual.

Fashionable – through observation, discussion with friends and your social media profile the Somatic Narcissist will be able to determine whether you are fashionable. He can see the shops you check in to or are photographed outside, he can view your outfits, the shoes and the accessories. He will take note of the car you drive, the way your house is furnished and what your friends wear also.

Shopping and gadgets - You will be followed around a mall to ascertain the places which you shop at. The frequency by which you post about your attendance at a particular café, one which is based in a shopping mall, confirms that you shop often. If necessary, post will be obtained to look through your credit card statements or bank statements to judge where you shop and the extent of your expenditure. Comments and photographs on social media will be examined for evidence of you having the latest coffee machine in your kitchen and largest television hanging on the wall of your living room. If we see you have been flying a drone through your tweets of the pictures taken when it has flown over your town, we will be pleased to see this interest you have in such gadgetry. If it is shiny, sleek and gleaming (just like us) we will be pleased to see that you have an interest in it.

Holidays – we will overhear holiday plans, use the Dating Lieutenant to find out how often you go on holiday, where you like to go and what you like to do on holiday. Is it wandering around ruins or lounging by the pool working on your tan? Social media will provide fantastic detail by way of photographs and where you have checked in to, tweeted from and Instagrammed about. We will be able to see if you have extensive holiday habits and of the variety which interests us.

Physical attraction - a personal viewing and an extensive perusal of your online photographs addresses this criterion.

Healthy Living & Beauty Products - again we will scrutinise your shopping habits for indicators of your use of such products and engagement with this way of living. We will observe what you eat in restaurants, get the Dating Lieutenants to tell us what you have ordered and also have them ask about your beauty routine, the products you use, how often you wear make-up, how often you wash your hair, whether you have hair extensions, have you had or would you have plastic surgery and if so what parts of your body would you change? Do you take vitamins and supplements? We may follow you whilst shopping to see what you purchase in terms of food and beauty products to ascertain if you fulfil this criterion.

Potential for Children – this is usually ascertained through contact or a dating Lieutenant may elicit this information too.

7.4 The Elite Narcissist

As you are aware, the Elite Narcissist is the combination of the Somatic and Cerebral Narcissists so he will be looking for those traits. He may not require them to quite the degree as those two would, but he will want to find evidence of them all. Accordingly, a prospective target who goes running and enjoys reading occasionally is entirely appropriate for the Elite Narcissist.

Leaders in Field - the Elite Narcissist will seek this confirmation from your friends through questioning and use the Dating Lieutenant to find out if you are a leader in your field. Social media will be heavily scrutinised, in particular LinkedIn in order to see if this criterion is fulfilled. Google searches will also be taken of your name to find press and media coverage of your achievements and reputation in order to see if you are a leader in a particular field and as such an attractive target for the Elite Narcissist.

Humour – the Elite Narcissist will scour your social media to see if your responses convey humour, whether you like certain comedians and the nature of memes and videos that you share. The Lieutenants will be used to draw out of you whether you have a sense of humour. Your film and reading preferences will also be studied for evidence of humour.

Challenging Individuals – If you regularly post on Facebook about depression or supporting those with personality disorders this will attract the attention of the Elite Narcissist. He will use a Lieutenant to follow you to your pharmacy and ascertain the details on your prescription so that the nature of the medication that you take can be considered and linked to an appropriate condition. Alternatively, we will recruit a Lieutenant from the doctor's reception staff or someone who works at the pharmacy in order to gain this information. We will ascertain from your friends whether you are regarded as independent, disciplined and strong-willed. If we see information on your social media about the level of exercise you engage in, the diet you are putting yourself though and similar we will recognise that you are likely to be strong-willed. We will check your comments on social media to see whether you are feisty, opinionated and unlikely to back down. We will find out if you live alone and how much interaction you have with family in terms of support in order to gauge your level of independence. Once again, through using the four main methods of background checks we will be able to ascertain whether you are a challenging individual and therefore worthy of our attention.

Gold-diggers – the Dating Lieutenant is a very useful way to find out if you are motivated by money. He will ascertain whether you like the finer things in life and what brands interest you. He will allow champagne to be ordered, the food will be a la carte and he will see if you make any offer to pay your share of the meal. He conversation will be steered towards money and prestige for most of the time to ascertain your reaction. We will listen in on your conversation with your friends in order to assess the extent to which you would like to be a kept woman. We may access financial information again to see if you have a high standard of living and perhaps you are living beyond your means. We will as usual check your social media for evidence of you making reference to status symbols and prestigious items.

Thus these are the varying ways in which we will ascertain whether you meet the relevant criteria. The four main methods are usually applied in each case. We learn information from your friends and this is particularly useful for ascertaining elements of your personality. We will use our Lieutenants to considerable effect in following you, peering into or gaining access to your home, questioning you under the pretext of a survey and most of all by taking you on a date and pumping you for information. Social media provides us with a wealth of information as you leave your footprint all across different platforms, demonstrating your likes, dislikes, attitudes and views, all of which we pay careful regard to and assimilate as we continue to assess your suitability as a target. Finally, we will rely on our own observation of you although you will never notice that we are doing it as we watch you and listen in on your conversations. There is so much material that we can accumulate through these four methods which tells us much about who you are but most of all whether you fulfil the criteria of the Generic and Class Traits. It is from this that we will decide whether we should move to the next stage of initiating contact so we can fine tune our work so far. Before that is done however we also consider, as part of the background checks whether you possess any of the special traits which will make you a very worthwhile target indeed.

8. The Special Traits

8.1 Gullible

A gullible individual is attractive to all narcissists. It makes them easier to seduce and easier to maintain a grip on. Ascertaining the gullibility of a target usually comes from when we make contact but it is feasible to get an idea from two sources; our Lieutenants and social media.

By organising for a Lieutenant to contact you with a suitable offer which sounds too good to be true we can ascertain how readily you are taken in. Alternatively, he will attend a date with you and make all manner of wild and flamboyant boasts about himself and see to what extent you challenge these declarations or whether you will accept them without question. He may begin by explaining that he is a fighter pilot and tell you about the sorties he has flown, even though he is wearing spectacles and therefore could not have been what he claims to be. He will make outlandish boasts about sporting and intellectual achievements but purposefully making a mistake and seeing if you pick up on it. He will move on to announce he is related to various famous people, that he played sport for his country and such like and note the extent by which you accept this without question or whether you challenge it.

The use of the Lieutenant is the most effective measure although we will also scour your social media for instances of gullibility where clear hoax material has been sent to you and you share it declaring it to be authentic or making comments which show that you do not questions something which is obviously the product of fakery. Your acceptance of things at face value is a trait which we look for since it means that all our outlandish boasts and behaviours will not be subjected to due diligence by you and will thus make your seduction all the easier.

8.2 Pleaser

The Pleaser is of particular interest to our kind as a consequence of their need to make other people feel comfortable and happy, ahead of their own needs. Such an individual is appealing to our kind as a consequence of the level of fuel that they will provide and also the fact that they are more likely to keep trying during a period of devaluation. You also want to be liked and therefore you will be pleasant and complimentary to other people in order to receive the same in return and if you do not, you are particularly hurt. This is a weakness which we exploit during both seduction (paying you lots of compliments which you want) and then during devaluation (by removing the compliments and making you feel bad about your behaviour towards us). The Pleaser will feel uncomfortable if they realise that someone else is unhappy and they will do anything they can to alleviate that sensation.

In determining whether a target will fulfil the Pleaser criterion we will place ourselves in a position where we can observe you. If we note that that you are fussing after everyone else, allowing other people to order before you, swapping seats because someone wanted to sit by the window where you are sat and allowing other people to speak ahead of you then there are indications that you may well be a Pleaser. We will listen to the conversations and if we note that you have a tendency to agree with what others are saying and you do not hold your own opinion on a matter we detect that you are a Pleaser. We will also look for whether you pay excessive compliments to others, whether you identify who the leader in the group is and suck up to them. We will watch for whether you say please and thank you a lot as excessive politeness is a sign of being a Pleaser. One key indicator is your capacity for apologising when it is not even your fault.

In common with other background checks we will use our Lieutenants. They will contact you and ask you questions, on the pretext of some kind of survey or research which consists of questions designed to elicit whether you are of a Pleaser personality.

By checking through your online postings we will identify these indicators from the way you interact with people, avoiding confrontation, doling out compliments and behaving in a similar way to the way we may see you act in the flesh.

8.3 **Susceptible to Manipulation**

Those of our targets who are particularly susceptible to manipulation are welcomed since quite obviously we will be able to conserve energy, seduce them more readily and then deploy our further manipulative mechanisms with greater ease. In terms of how we identify somebody who has this Special Trait then through a combination of observation, liaison with your friends, trawling your social media and deploying our Lieutenants we will be looking for: -

- Inability to make a decision
- Changing mind
- Having no firm opinion about various subjects
- Low self-esteem
- People who respond quickly to situations and messages without thinking them through. They place speed over accuracy and this leads to poor decision making.
- Inability to say no
- Over emotional (which again leads to poor decision making)
- Those who respond to anchoring. This is where they seize on the first part of information we give them and focus too strongly on it causing them to accept a position which is worse for them even though they believe it is better for them. An example of this would be let us say we wish to manipulate you into wearing something unsuitable for a night out when we

are not attending. You parade an outfit in front of you and we respond by telling you that you look fat in the outfit and point a different one instead (which actually looks worse than the one you had on). Such a person would be hurt by the remark and so concerned by it, they do not challenge whether they look fat or not but instead accept the alternative without proper consideration as to its suitability because they wish to alleviate their discomfort at being told they look fat in the other outfit. Someone who falls prey to anchoring is someone who is susceptible to being manipulated.

- People who are overly trusting

These indicators can be found in your behaviour. We may come across an exchange between you and your friends on Facebook or Twitter where you are discussing where you might go out that evening and we see you cannot commit to a decision, then follow someone else's decision but then change your mind when other people suggest an alternative. Similarly, we may see a post whereby you remark that you are tired and want your bed. A friend posts that they want you to come out and after a little pleading, you agree. Similarly, we see you accept at face value certain items which are evidently fake which do the rounds on social media.

A lieutenant may spill a drink on you. In fact, this is a common tactic that I have my lieutenants deploy when ascertaining the reaction of the person who has just had a glass of wine or beer tipped over them seemingly on accident.

"You idiot, look what you've done, you are paying for the dry cleaning, Jesus, what an arsehole."

Too aggressive and hostile.

"It's done now, no I will mop it up, but you can buy me a drink by way of apology."

Assertive and expressing independence, therefore may fulfil challenging person criterion.

"Oh my God, what have you done, this top is brand new, it is ruined, oh no, my night is ruined (bursts into tears)"
Nearly histrionic response, overly emotional and therefore potentially an individual susceptible to manipulation.

"Oh I am sorry, was I in the way, here, no it is okay, let me get you another drink, it must have been my fault."
A Pleaser.

The variance of responses to this sudden act so there is an immediate response rather than a carefully considered one provides us with useful insight into your character and thus allows information to be gleaned about your ability to fulfil certain criteria. It also provides an immediate in for the Lieutenant to remain talking to you and the group to find out more information. The spilled drink routine is something I often use through a lieutenant.

8.4 Damaged

The damaged individual often encompasses the first three special traits and therefore is a prize find for our kind. Ascertaining this special criterion is somewhat harder at the background stage. Observation does not allow us to witness its existence and questioning your friends will not yield the information either, it is too personal and sensitive to reveal at such an early juncture. Lieutenants may make some headway on a date but they are likely only going to be provided with snippets which may hint at the target being damaged. After all, they will be trying to show their best side to my Lieutenant and may look to keep such information under wraps. Social media is the key to ascertaining the indicators for this special trait. We look for your membership of certain support groups (indeed we will infiltrate those groups as a hunting ground), we look for posts about how you are feeling and especially those supposed supportive and uplifting quotes against a backdrop of some flowers or a cloud. If we see you have posted number of those quotes and you regularly make mention of how down you feel, how you miss a certain person and such like then there is a strong indicator that you are damaged which will attract our attention so that we decide to move to the next stage which is initiating contact with you.

9 Contact

With our background checks undertaken through the main four methods of doing so we will have ascertained whether you have sufficient potential as a target by checking off what we have learned for (and been specifically looking for) about your compatibility with the Generic Traits, Class Traits and where possible the Special Traits. We will decide that contact is now appropriate (i.e. our time is unlikely to be wasted) and we will be making a final check as to your suitability as a target and easing our self into your environment. We will be ascertaining your continued and further suitability against the trait checklists and will engineer an opportunity to do so by having face to face contact with you. We are looking for what I refer to as the green lights which indicate that you will be an excellent primary source and thus seduction can begin. Obviously, this method of gauging your suitability and seeking for these green lights relies on being in your presence. Accordingly, I am going to provide you with some worked examples of how I do this in practice and so you can see the type of things that are done, what is said and why as you remain in my sights and I firm you up as the right target for my forthcoming seduction. I highlight relevant observations in the course of the examples.

The Cerebral Narcissist at the Museum

Background - a target has been identified who I have seen attend a military museum on a number of occasions. A Lieutenant was able to ascertain from the staff at the museum the name of the target. This allowed her to be identified on social media. She operates a twitter account in her name and also has a Facebook account. I followed her on twitter using a profile which does not identify who I am. A Lieutenant struck up a messenger conversation with her and was added as a friend. Through this Lieutenant's access I have reviewed her postings, photographs, interests and likes and numerous criteria in the Cerebral and Generic Traits have been matched. I am aware that she has a particular interest in Prussian history and she has a cat named Oscar. She is a target prospect so it is time to find out more by engaging with her. I have observed her as well and noticed she always goes to the museum every fortnight on a Sunday and then likes to sit in the café and read after she has looked around. She always attends on her own and has been making notes in a large Black and Red notebook which she carries with her. She is in the café and I position myself at an adjoining table. I see she is reading a Clockwork Orange by Anthony Burgess.

I regard her for a moment and note she does not wear an engagement or wedding ring. She wears a little make-up but not a lot. She is of a willowy frame **(Not physically strong)** and quite attractive with blue eyes and long brown hair. I see a newspaper (a quality broadsheet) **(Current affairs)** tucked in to her bag.

"What do you think of the novel?"
"Oh I have read it a couple of times before but I always enjoy it," she answers with a smile. **(Reading)**
"Yes I have read it probably half a dozen times. As it is usually the case, I prefer the book to the film."

"I agree. I think it is probably because the film now looks dated and also since Kubrick would not allow it to be shown for so long the violence contained in it has become rather tame by today's standards."

"Yes, it seems rather cartoon like doesn't it?"

"Yes it does. The book is far more visceral." **(Intellectual Capability)**

"Absolutely, I also found some of the changes made in the film a little bewildering. After all, in the book the person murdered by Alex is an old lady yet in the film Kubrick knocked twenty years off her age and had her living in a sex museum for some reason."

She laughs at my comment and places the book down.

"May I join you?" I ask indicating to her table.

"By all means," she responds. **(Sociable)**

I sit at right angles to her, perhaps slightly closer than one would ordinarily do so and she does not move back. **(Positive body language).**

We talk for a while longer about the book. We debate the need for punishment against the fact that Alex's free will has been taken from and therefore he cannot choose to do good or bad. **(Intellectual capability)** She expresses concern for this and that she found his manipulation by the government distasteful. **(Underdog)** She does not think it appropriate that this should be done and instead she believes that the root of his offending should be examined **(Compassionate)** and he should be provided with help to overcome what was probably a difficult childhood. **(Caring)** I notice when she refers to difficulties in childhood that her tone of voice alters. **(Damaged).** I notice that her coffee mug is empty and I offer to purchase her another which she accepts. She offers me payment but I decline **(Decent).** I noted that her mobile 'phone was on the table and she did not look at it once whilst we talked even when it lit up several times with notifications or messages **(Decent) (Excellent Listener).** During the conversation I pointed out that Burgess was actually a linguist (she did not know this) and that his invented language nadsat which the anti-hero Alex uses in his narration and interaction with others is a combination of English, Russian, German and Cockney rhyming slang. She was unaware of that also and expressed interest and delight in learning of this **(Likes knowledge)**. I know from her social media that reading dystopian novels is something that she enjoys.

"I should imagine, "I explained, "that if you like a Clockwork Orange then you will enjoy 1984 and Brave New World?"

"Oh absolutely, you see choice is another thing that is removed from individuals when they are placed into the relevant castes in Brave New World," she responds.

(Reading)

I then embarked on a lengthy discourse about the parallels between the alpha to epsilon semi-moron castes with our society and she listened attentively. **(Excellent listener).** Our conversation then veered towards politics **(Interest in the wider world)** and she made reference to her concerns about the bridge between the rich and poor and the issues surrounding the appropriate taxation of multinationals **(Moral compass)**. I then steered the conversation to her interest in Prussian military history.

"So how long have you been visiting the museum?" I asked

"Oh years, it really is an impressive place."

"Yes it is. I like to come here most weeks."

"Are you interested in anything in particular?" she asked.

"Well I like a lot of the medieval displays, early medieval but I also have a keen interest in Prussian military history."

"No? Really?" she expresses surprise and delight and in doing so places a hand on my arm. **(Positive body language)**

"Oh yes, I particularly like King Frederick the Great and his campaigns during the Silesian Wars, he was a formidable commander."

"You won't believe it but I adore Prussian military history, I am undertaking research as part of a thesis for my master's degree."

"Oh do you study full-time?"

"No I am director in a social housing organisation **(Decent)(Caring)(Underdog)** but I am studying it part-time. Fancy you liking the same subject as well."

"Absolutely, it is a very interesting subject to analyse. I noticed you carry a note book, is that for your thesis?"

"Yes it is."

"May I have a look?"

"Sure, it is a lot of notes but some ideas and theories too," she smiles and hands me the notebook. I leaf through it and pass the occasional comment on what I read so far as I am able within the confines of the rudimentary background information I have committed to memory about this particular subject. I allow her to espouse one of her theories about the influence of the Thirty Years' War on the origins of Prussian military ascent as I flick through her notebook and find what I am looking for. Her home address written at the front of the note book with a request for the book to be returned there if it is found. I make a note of the address in my mind.

We talk about further books, films and also she mentions her cat explaining she took him from a rescue shelter **(Interest in films and plays) (Compassionate) (Decent)** and it is evident from the way that she talks she lives alone. I politely ask about that and she confirms she does live alone and prefers that as it gives her time to think and do the things that she enjoys. I have determined that she has clearly engaged with me and that she has matched many Generic and Cerebral Traits and there is a suggestion of a Special Trait also. I also have noted several green lights in her behaviour: -

- She immediately engaged in conversation with me
- She made no move to end the conversation, in fact I made an excuse about having to meet a friend for lunch and I could see she was slightly disappointed I had to go

- Her body language throughout was positive in terms of showing me attention
- She freely provided information to me and was not hesitant or guarded

Based on all of this I conclude that she is a viable target and ask if we might go for dinner. She agrees and numbers are exchanged. My seduction can now begin.

The Somatic Narcissist and the Bar

Background – I frequent a bar called Tokyo which has been open about six months. It is reasonably expensive, has a VIP section and is often busy and is frequented by the beautiful and the young. A very attractive red-head has caught my attention. I have seen her in the bar on three occasions. Questioning of the barman and a hefty tip revealed her name and that she is a regular. I learn from the barman two of the names of her friends also. She is very easy to find on social media as she has accounts with Facebook, Twitter, Snapchat and Instagram. Her postings are all about where she has been out, where she would like to go and many pictures of her and her friends. I note she has been to Puerto Banus a number of times and has remarked about her desire to go to Dubai. She is a receptionist at a law firm. Numerous criteria have been established and you appear to be a good target prospect so I decide to make my move and initiate contact.

I walk towards her from the bar. I nudge into her and cause her to spill her full cocktail glass so some of the contents land on her short skirt. She lets out a surprised cry and I turn to her.
"Sorry about that," I remark.
She is mopping at the liquid as one of her friends pulls a tissue from her bag.
"It is okay, my fault, it is too busy here, we shouldn't be stood here really but the bar is packed," she answers **(Pleaser)**
"No it is my fault, I wasn't looking where I was going. Please, let me buy you a drink. In fact," I say looking at her three friends, "let me buy all you lovely ladies a drink." All four smile and issue their thanks. **(Positive response to largesse)**
"In fact, seeing as it is so busy here, why don't you come and sit with us? There's plenty of room in our booth, we are in VIP?"
"Oh yes please," you announce and I lead all four of you over to where I am sat with a Lieutenant and two members of my coterie. **(Sociable)** I usher you ahead

allowing me to admire your figure. **(Physically attractive).** You are well dressed in a short skirt and tight top. Your red tresses spill down your back and you wear jewellery around your neck, wrists, ears and fingers. **(Fashionable).** Your clutch bag is red leather and with Moschino emblazoned across it in gold lettering. It is probably cost two or three hundred pounds and is not commensurate with your likely earnings as a receptionist, even in a law firm. **(Shopping).**

    I ensure you sit next to me in the booth and you are pressed up against me but make no attempt to move **(Positive body language)**. Introductions are effected and I learn your name (although of course I already know it) I converse to the group at large, giving every equal attention and you sit and listen with butting in allowing other people to talk **(Pleaser) (Good listener)** and I then focus on you allowing the other members of my group to occupy your friends.

"So then Rebecca or do you prefer Becky?"

"Becca actually."

"Fair enough."

"Looking at you I would say you are a Capricorn?"

You smile and open your mouth. **(Gullible)**

"How do you know that?"

"Oh I can tell you are a hard worker when you are in work, you know down-to-earth but you know how to enjoy yourself. Let me guess, I would say you are either an air hostess or the head receptionist somewhere important."

"Can you mind read or something? I am the head reception at Sue Grabbit and Runn" you respond.

"The law firm? Yes, I know them, good firm."

"Have you used them?" you ask.

"No but my company was on the other side in some litigation. I don't know the ins and outs of it all but my md said your firm was decent enough. I am not really into all that legal stuff, are you?"

"Lord no, I mean, I know where to direct queries too and so on but I am not into all that. Far too much reading, I would rather be out and about." **(No real interest in books)**

"Yes, I much prefer that, I have seen you here a few times before actually, I always wanted to chat with you though."

"Really? How come?"

"You seem like a nice person and fun."

"Oh I am that alright," you laugh and hold my gaze. **(Positive body language)**

"I like your rings, let me see?" I ask and take your hand. You do not resist. **(Positive body language).** I note there are no rings denoting engagement or marriage.

"Not hitched then?" I ask tapping your finger but still holding your hand.

"No, fancy free and footloose."

"What not even a boyfriend?"

"No, we split up a year ago, I have been on dates but not found the right person yet."

"So you are looking then?"

"Oh yes, always looking, there is someone right for us all out there, it is just a question of time as to when it happens," you remark. **(Love devotee)**

"Oh absolutely."

"Do you have a girlfriend?"

"Not yet," I smile and she responds with her own smile **(Positive body language)**

"I would like one, I am due to go to Dubai in a month and I would like to have somebody go there with me."

"Dubai? You lucky thing, I would love to go there I have never been."

"You like going on holiday?"

"Yes, I do. I try and go as often as I can. I go to Puerto Banus a lot. My mum and dad live in Marbella and my dad is getting on so I like to go and check they are okay; you know?" **(Caring) (Holidays)**

"Sure, it is difficult when you are a distance away from your family. I like Puerto Banus. I like the Navy Bar, my father was in the navy so we go in there when we visit." (He wasn't but I recall the target has been in that bar a few times from her postings).

"Yes I like that one too. I have been a few times."

We continue talking and I take you on the usual tour ascertaining the things you like in terms of films (you like romantic comedies and chick flicks **(Love devotee)**) and you talk about shopping and the things you like to purchase **(Shopping) (Beauty products).** I ask more about your previous relationship and you explain it did not work out even though you did your best to do make it work **(Pleaser).** You explain that he cheated on you and you caught him out after you became suspicious about his behaviour. **(Strives for the truth)** You show a degree of upset about it but steady yourself. **(Love devotee).** You tell me more about your work and I learn that you are in charge of looking after the law firm's juniors in a pastoral role which was something you suggested to the firm and they agreed that should be implemented. **(Compassionate) (Decent)** I notice you offer to buy me a drink even though I have been ordering champagne for everyone and I thank you but decline. You are effusive in your thanks for letting you sit in the booth as you have always wanted to "do VIP" **(Pleaser) (Decent)**

When you go to the toilet you say excuse me **(Decent)** and whilst you are gone one of your friends leans in and tells me what a good person you are and that you need someone kind and decent to look after you after what you have been through. She tells no more but there is a suggestion of some kind or incident or trauma which will be worth investigating **(Damaged).**

Green lights have been established during the conversation and time spent together as follows: -

- Positive body language
- Ready acceptance to spend time with us
- Content to divulge information about yourself
- No desire to leave my company
- Several 'hits' in the Special Trait category

Whilst you have been to the bathroom I have established that you match many of the Generic and Somatic Criteria which are applicable to the type of person I want as a target and moreover there is a strong showing by you in respect of Special Trait compliance. I begin my seduction on your return and later that night your return to my house with me.

The Victim Narcissist and the Medical Centre

Background - The Victim Narcissist frequents a same-day medical centre using it as his main hunting ground. He suffers from gout and makes repeated visits based on this affliction but also trawls the internet for various "invisible" complaints that he can bring to the attention of the staff there. He has observed one particular nurse that works at the medical centre who he has an interest in because he was at school with her and therefore has a crucial existing connection that he wishes to exploit. He has established already the target's name and ascertained where she lives by having her followed to her house by a Lieutenant. She is single and has a child. There has not been any evidence so far of a significant other. She takes the bus to work as your Lieutenant has followed her to the bus stop and followed her on the bus to the relevant stop at the other end. Her social media profile is limited to Facebook. There is not much information posted on it as she is not a frequent poster and what is posted is in the main information related to fund raising for a diabetes charity and occasional expressions of 'happy birthday' to the small group of friends which she has on Facebook.

Using a Lieutenant, the Victim Narcissist as established when the target's shift patterns are. The same day centre closes at 10pm. The VN has made an appointment for 9-45 pm when he knows there are only two nurses available and therefore he has maximised his prospects of being seen by the target. His planning is successful and she emerges from her room to call him over.

The VN limps across from the waiting room and the target waits with a pleasant smile om her face displaying no evidence of the long and testing shift that she has experienced. **(Decent)**
"Do you want to take my arm, you seem to be struggling somewhat there," she remarks. **(Caring)**

The VN accepts her arm and limps along to her room. Once inside he is seated.
"Back again Mr VN eh?
"Yes, a few things today nurse, the old gout is giving me trouble, so I my back and I have been getting these dizzy spells as well."
"Oh dear, falling apart at the seams aren't you my dear, well let's see how I can help you. That gout must be painful judging by the way you walk. I know many people laugh about it thinking it is from drinking too much port and eating stilton but I know it is not funny, it is very painful and you don't have to be a fat old man to suffer from it, I have had all manner of different people here who suffer from it, so I understand." **(Compassionate)**
The VN goes on at length about his symptoms, providing a detailed recollection of what has been happening, when it hurts and how often in respect of all of his complaint. The target listens patiently despite the approaching closure of the centre and does not hurry him. **(Decent) (Excellent listener)**
The target's manner is pleasant and soothing as she removes his shoes and sock for him to examine the afflicted toes. She carefully examines them and is delicate and tender in her movements. **(Consummate care giver)**
The VN watches her carefully. She is only short in height, a little on the heavy side and unremarkable in looks **(Physically weaker)**
During the examination the target fusses about the VN not looking after himself properly concerning his admission he drinks a lot of fruit juice which exacerbating his condition. She checks on his back making suitable sympathies noises when he issues noise of pain when trying to move. **(Mothering) (Caring)**
"I went to school with you, "remarks the VN as the target makes some notes.
"Yes I know, I didn't know whether you would recognise me or not, I am a bit older than back then," she laughs.
"Oh I recognised you straight away, you don't look that much older, not like me, I have had a hard paper round," comments the VN.
"Oh you charmer," she laughs.

"Now I want to run a few checks on you concerning these dizzy spells as they do worry me a little Mr VN, so I am going to check your blood pressure, take some blood and do you think you will be able to have a pee for me?" **(Needs to understand)**

The VN nods.

"Have you been doing this since school?" he asks.

"No I worked in a supermarket for a while and then shops. I didn't study hard enough at school although I wish I had so I left with only a few qualifications." **(Honest) (Not a high achiever)**

"But I went to night school and then studied nursing and here I am."

"You have done well."

"I enjoy it. It is hard work and the pay could be better but you don't do it for that do you? I like being with people and getting to know them. I have a lot of regular patients and I feel like their family after a while. They tell you all sorts when they are sat in here." **(Companionship) (Not interested in money/status) (Giver not receiver)**

"Yes I bet this place keeps you pretty busy, plenty of patients out there."

"Yes there are. Now pop this on your arm," she smiles as she begins to take his blood pressure.

"You have a kiddy haven't you? I seem to remember John Robinson telling me, I bumped into him a month or two back on the High Street."

"Yes, a little girl, Rosie." **(Children)**

"Lovely name. How old is she?"

"Nine."

"Bet she keeps you busy?"

"Oh yes, between her and this place I don't have much time for anything else, but that's what I like doing you know." **(Few outside interests)**

The target continues with her work and arranges for tests to be run on the relevant samples provided whilst she provides some medication to assist with the gout and back pain. It is 10-15 pm by the time she has finished but did not demonstrate any desire to hurry the VN out of the centre. **(Decent)** Outside it is raining and the VN offers a lift to the target in light of the lateness of the hour and the foul weather. At first she refuses saying she is content to get the bus but the VN points out that it is the least he can do after her help and she agrees. **(Decent)**

The VN has identified green lights: -

- Willingness to remain and treat him despite over-running
- Acceptance of lift home
- Willingness to talk to him
- Lack of judgement about his conditions (since two are made-up)

This provision of the lift home provides him with further opportunity to learn more through talking with her and during this journey he decides that she satisfies many of the things which he regards as important namely the Generic Traits and Victim Traits so that he gauges her to be viable target. By way of thanking him for the lift and the fact she enjoyed the homebound conversation (the VN settled on topics of family and caring and also managed to get her to tell him about her cake baking) she invited the VN in for a mug of cocoa. He readily accepted and in the course of being a guest he purposefully spilt the cocoa on himself in order to elicit a further mothering and caring response from the target as he began to slide his tendrils towards her.

The Elite Narcissist and the Gala Dinner

I found you in a support group online for those who suffer with anxiety. I made no contact with you but watched and silently observed as you posted many comments that told me much about yourself. I learned that you enjoy running as it helps relieve your anxiety, I found out two of your favourite television programmes which you post about when engaging in discussions with other members of the group, I ascertained you like to write poetry since you post some of your efforts for other group members to look at. I followed you in some other guise on twitter and it was there that I ascertained that you have a diagnosis of borderline personality disorder. I did not send you a friend request but arranged for a Lieutenant to join the anxiety group. He did so and engaged with you and you sent him a friend request which he accepted. My suspicions from what you had posted confirmed that you were based in the same city and further online investigations revealed that you were involved in organising a gala ball to promote awareness of a specific charity which carries out work with those suffering from anxiety. I arrange for my Lieutenant to suggest donating certain prizes to the raffle and auction and purely platonically he secured taking you to the ball. He also suggested arranging a further sponsor who just happened to be me and offered my services to conduct the auction at the ball as it is something I have done previously. You were only too delighted to receive this assistance and further financial help. The discussions between you and the Lieutenant and the online observations have demonstrated that you satisfy numerous of the important traits and as a consequence I decide I will make contact at the gala ball. I conduct the auction and keep looking to you throughout the auction, gaining your attention and it is clear your admiration from you and of course the remainder of the audience which is all good fuel for me as I home in on my target. I later join you at the bar where you are stood with my Lieutenant. He melts away on my arrival.

"Well that seemed to go down very well," I remark.

"Absolutely, you were brilliant, thank you so so much for doing it. We were let down late on by the man who normally does it. I think he was double-booked. So good of you to do it for nothing as well, we normally have to pay. You are an absolute saint. I loved the jokes you threw in as well, the other fellow is a bit dry, but you gauged it just right, you were hilarious." **(Pleaser) (Humour)**

"Oh I could not accept money not from such a worthwhile event as this. Peter (my Lieutenant) tells me you have been involved in the charity for quite a while?"

"Yes that is right, about eight years now, I am a trustee as well."

"Magnificent, I am impressed. Given how demanding the world is these days I am always impressed by those who give up their time for such worthwhile causes. There is so much selfishness and a me, me, me attitude these days."

"Oh I agree," you answer.

I embark on a detailed analysis of why people are so self-centred and you listen attentively as I speak. **(Excellent listener)**. You agree with everything I say, nodding and making confirmatory noises **(Pleaser)**.

"So, what drew you to the charity then? Did it just appeal to you or have you had to look after someone who suffers from anxiety?" I ask.

"I am a sufferer and the charity helped me greatly," you explain.

"Really? You seem so composed and confident, I would never have thought it?"

"Thank you that is kind of you, inside I was churning before the event and I could never stand up there and do what you do, I would go to pieces. "**(Honest)**

"Nonsense, anybody can do that, it is just a gift of the gab really," I smile.

"You are being modest"

"Look, let's get another drink and sit over here so we aren't in people's way and you can tell me more about how you got involved," I suggest. You agree and we sit down to one side so I have you to myself. You tell me about your anxiety and also your diagnosis of BPD, I feign ignorance and ask more about it in order to understand. I make suitably sympathetic noises as you tell me your life story, providing me with a raft of detail **(Honest) (Challenging Individuals) (Damaged) (Susceptible to manipulation)**

I change tack and compliment you on your dress and how well you look **(Physically attractive)** and we continue to converse as I learn more about your interests which include travel **(Holidays)** and how much you enjoy going to the cinema and theatre **(Films and plays)**. You hold the conversation well and touch on a variety of issues linked to the government's stance with mental health and how you would like to do more campaigning **(Intellectual capability) (Current affairs) (Interest in the wider world) (Strives for the truth) (Underdog)** and I sit listening as I note the various green lights which have lit up

- Disclosure of intimate and personal information very readily
- Willingness to be cornered
- Positive body language throughout
- No desire to end conversation

I conclude that you are a most viable prospect as you match many criteria for the Somatic, Cerebral, Elite, Generic and Special Traits. I decide that my seduction will now begin and make my first move by suggesting that my business has more involvement with the charity and arranging to have dinner with you to discuss this in more detail and to get to know one another better. You happily agree and you are most effusive in your thanks as a tendril slides around your middle.

You will note that when we make contact with our target we will steer the conversation into areas that allow us to establish whether the criteria are being met. You may think that we are expressing an interest in you and being friendly and polite but we are intent on conducting our fact finding in order to establish your suitability. We are also observing the way you behave and the things you do as we pick up further hints as to your traits from these actions and your body language as well. It is extremely rare for the subject to feel that they are being questioned unnecessarily and the target never realises that they are being assessed in that fashion to determine their suitability as a target. It may appear as if the seduction has already begun but we are still very much in the assessment stage although it would be wrong to deny that the bridges to your heart have begun construction. By ensuring we meet with you we can make those judgements about you and assess in particular how you respond to our presence so that the various green lights and then the seduction begins.

10 Conclusion

You no doubt recognise what is was about you that made the narcissist choose you now you have read this book. We are structured and methodical about the way we go about choosing you and the reason why is always geared to our need to obtain fuel from both a primary source and supplementary sources. Our initial considerations revolve around the type of narcissist that we are, which school and which cadre we hail from influences who we choose as our target. We next consider the role that the target will fulfil. Is this person to join the growing ranks of our supplementary sources or are we looking for that special primary source? Naturally, the latter requires greater consideration and effort to ensure that he or she makes the grade to accomplish this important role.

The primary source is nearly always an intimate partner and this is why their eventual seduction must be based on the soundest of foundations. We will be spending much time with them and seeking much fuel from them. The supplementary sources come from all other types of proximity of supply. We look for the traits in those individuals, although the lower the rank of proximity of supply the fewer of the traits are required since the effort in ascertaining those traits will not equate to the fuel we will draw from them. Our need is fuel and thus we look, especially in the primary source, for those who fit the criteria relevant to the Generic, Class and Special Traits. The more traits that the prospect matches the better the target they are. The Generic Traits must always be present in at least one or more forms because they are central to the provision of fuel and they also provide a residual benefit to us.

Knowing what we are looking for in terms of the fuel potential from those who match the various traits means that only certain people in society become eligible as targets. The class of target is important as we scour the populace looking for normal people, empaths, super empaths and co-dependents. We have established hunting grounds where the people we need and with the appropriate traits are most likely to be found and you should have careful regard to those that you meet within those hunting grounds lest they be one of our brethren.

With our needs established, our hunting ground visited and our class of target identified it is all then about how we target you by first undertaking preparatory work. Our background checks through the four main channels of using your friends, deploying our Lieutenants, scouring social media and observation enable us to determine your suitability or otherwise by reference to the traits. We have a raft of ways by which we are able to make this assessment so that our time and energy is not wasted in pursuing the wrong type of target. With the results of the background checks providing us with helpful indicators it is time for us to introduce ourselves to you and make contact. This contact and the further gathering of information to check against the traits can take place in a number of ways but the aim is always the same; we want to ensure that you are the right target. We look for those green lights which confirm that you are the correct target and will fulfil the role that we have identified for you. Once that has been done we are satisfied that you are a viable target and thus the seduction can begin as out tendrils snake towards you ready to draw you in and begin the extraction of that sweet and delicious fuel.

You now know why and how we target you. You are better armed to avoid being caught a second or third time. You are better placed to advise those you care about and love what they should look for and watch out for in order to avoid remaining a sitting target. Oh and always think before you respond if someone spills a drink on you, you never know who it might be.

Further reading from H G Tudor

Evil

Narcissist: Seduction

Narcissist: Ensnared

Manipulated

Confessions of a Narcissist

More Confessions of a Narcissist

Further Confessions of a Narcissist

From the Mouth of a Narcissist

Escape: How to Beat the Narcissist

Danger: 50 Things You Should Not Do with a Narcissist

Departure Imminent: Preparing for No Contact to beat the Narcissist

Fuel

Chained: The Narcissist's Co-Dependent

A Delinquent Mind

Fury

Beautiful and Barbaric

The Devil's Toolkit

Sex and the Narcissist

Treasured and Tormented

No Contact: How to Beat the Narcissist

Revenge: How to Beat the Narcissist

Adored and Abhorred

All available on Amazon

Further interaction with H G Tudor

Knowing the Narcissist

@narcissist_me

Facebook

Narcsite.wordpress.com

Made in the USA
San Bernardino, CA
19 January 2017